Strengthening the Capacity of NGOs:

Cases of Small Ent Development Agen Africa

Caroline Sahley

INTRAC

INTRAC NGO Management and Policy Series

INTRAC:
Supporting the development of NGOs internationally

A SUMMARY DESCRIPTION
set up in 1991 to provide specially designed Management Training & Research
Services for European NGOs involved in relief and development in the South and
dedicated to improving organisational effectiveness and programme performance of
Northern NGOs and Southern partners where appropriate.

Our goal is to serve NGOs in (i) the exploration of the management, policy and
human resource issues affecting their own organisational development, and (ii) the
evolution of more effective programmes of institutional development and
cooperation.

INTRAC offers the complementary services of
Training,
Consultancy
and Research

Within three themes
(1) NGO Management and Organisation
(2) Improving Development Projects and Programmes
(3) Media Management and Policy Advocacy

INTRAC is supported by the Aga Khan Foundation, UK

INTRAC
PO Box 563
Oxford
UK

338.966
(t)

Telephone: +44 (0)1865 201851
Fax: +44 (0)1865 201852

Designed & produced by
Davies Burman Associates

Printed in Great Britain
Reprinted in August 1997
ISBN 1 897748 10 8

Contents

Foreword

This book makes a practical and timely contribution to the current debate on capacity building and organisational development for NGOs. Although the case material is taken from Africa, the principles evolved in these pages are of more universal interest and significance to all development practitioners. The book builds upon the foundations laid in INTRAC's earlier study of institutional development in Africa (Fowler *et al.* 1992), which has become a benchmark study for those involved in development work with NGOs worldwide. This current study on capacity building for small enterprise development agencies can be recommended not only to readers in this field, but also for those interested in different aspects of capacity building with NGOs.

The present book grew out of an INTRAC initiative to explore the nature of small enterprise development in Africa. It had become clear that UK NGOs had a growing interest in supporting small enterprise development programmes in Africa. In researching the approaches most appropriate to the needs of African countries it was discovered that both the literature and experience of most 'international experts' was dominated by the work of enterprise development programmes in Latin America and Asia. INTRAC therefore decided to explore the experience of NGOs in Africa through a series of workshops held in the UK. In 1994, we held 4 workshops covering difference aspects of enterprise development, including credit, marketing and training, gender, and capacity building. These workshops benefited from the contributions from UK NGOs such as Care, Traidcraft Exchange, Intermediate Technology Development Group, Womankind Worldwide, Durham University Business School, as well as from experienced enterprise development practitioners from Kenya, Zimbabwe, South Africa, Kenya, Egypt, Ghana and Niger.

In trying to isolate some of the factors important in developing sustainable enterprise development programmes, we realised that more general principles were involved which hold good for other types of programmes and in different contexts. By the time we reached the last workshop in the series it became clear that one of the issues of primary concern was the organisational capacity and sustainability of African agencies implementing enterprise development programmes. It was therefore decided to devote the present book less to the mechanisms of specific credit, marketing or training small enterprise programmes but to concentrate upon the wider issue of capacity building. By strengthening local NGOs, greater impact can be achieved by developing sustainable programmes capable of reaching significant numbers of micro- and small businesses, hence assisting entrepreneurs to improve their incomes and general livelihoods. INTRAC is grateful to the support from the ODA Small Enterprise Fund for its support, and would like to thank David Wright and Richard Boulter for their individual participation at the four workshops. We are pleased at the positive response of the UK NGO community to the workshop series and would like to thank the many people who attended the workshops in different capacities and contributed to the overall programme.

Brian Pratt
Executive Director, INTRAC
Oxford 6/95

Preface

Many of the more notable and celebrated experiences of large-scale small enterprise development programmes are found in Asia and Latin America. The Grameen Bank in Bangladesh has had particular exposure and is often heralded as the best example of a large-scale credit delivery system as a result of its impressive reach and cost recovery success. Similarly, in Latin America, innovative experiences with formal financial linkages and village banking methods have been developed. These programmes have had a considerable impact on the evolution of theory and practice of enterprise development.

Examples of influential and innovative African enterprise development programmes are harder to come by. The current study originates from a demand for good case study materials of small enterprise development programmes in Africa. This research and workshop programme launched by INTRAC in 1994 sought to address the relative shortage of published analyses of enterprise development in Africa.

It emerged from our debates at the workshops that the key issue arising from the case studies was the long-term prospects for the organisational sustainability of the small enterprise development agencies themselves. It is true that a growing number of enterprise development agencies operating credit programmes in Africa have been demonstrating impressive financial successes. As financial sustainability becomes within reach of more agencies, however, a deeper and possibly more intractable problem is surfacing: that of the long-term organisational sustainability of the implementing NGOs. The effective transfer of credit programme management to fully autonomous local control is one of the key challenges facing Northern NGOs. It is often assumed or implied in NGO project proposals and evaluations that financial sustainability will lead to organisational sustainability. While financial sustainability may be a necessary precondition, it is certainly not a sufficient precondition.

The goal of Northern NGO 'exit' and devolution to local agencies is particularly problematic in Africa, where there is an incipient and poorly institutionalised local NGO sector. These issues are currently being tackled through capacity building and organisational development programmes for Southern NGOs. The key for genuine sustainability lies in the capacity of local service providers. As a result, intensive management training and support is now being redirected, away from the entrepreneurs themselves, to the local implementing agencies. Capacity building programmes that enhance the administrative and managerial capacity of NGOs and enable them to adapt successfully to growth and change will therefore need to play an important role in the development strategies of Northern NGOs and donors.

INTRAC would like to thank the Small Enterprise Fund at the ODA for supporting this work and the accompanying workshop series that explored various aspects of enterprise development and organisational development. These workshops provided a valuable opportunity for British and African NGOs to come together to share their insights, experiences, successes and failures. It also, we hope, helped to initiate a new atmosphere of cooperation and dialogue amongst NGOs on small enterprise development issues.

Thanks are owed to the NGOs that allowed their case studies to be used for publication. The following people were helpful in providing access to project files and information, and in answering seemingly endless questions: Paul Bradnum, Triple Trust Organisation; Simon Matsvai, Symacon; Wilbert Tengey, The African Centre for Human Development; Chris Sealy, APT Design and Development; Patrick Sayer, Care Britain; and Will Day and Lucy Charrington, The Opportunity Trust.

As with any research programme, many people contributed to making this publication possible. A deep debt of gratitude is owed to Catherine Sahley and Elizabeth Stamp for many days spent patiently editing the first draft. In Africa, thanks must go to the staff of numerous enterprise development agencies in Ghana and Kenya. Many individuals took time away from their busy schedules to take me on field visits to observe their programmes and always offered a warm and hospitable welcome. In the UK, special thanks to Malory Greene, Katarina Dalacoura and my colleagues at INTRAC, (Alex Jeffs, Leo Thomas, Sara Gibbs, Paul Ryder, Liz Goold, Adrian Stone, and Andy Clayton), for their cheerful support and advice. I owe a particular debt to Brian Pratt, John Hailey, Alan Fowler, Piers Campbell and Rick James, who at INTRAC have spent many years exploring, debating and advancing the issues of management and organisational development for NGOs. This publication draws on much of the material they have developed for INTRAC training courses, and they must be justly credited as the intellectual pioneers in this field. The task of synthesizing debates and writing the manuscript was conducted in Cleveland, Ohio, where Jake, Brant, Martina, Regina and all at Maplecrest and West Sixth, offered their friendship and encouragement. This book, however, is dedicated to Mom, Dad, Cathy, Teddy and Mery, for their unwavering support and enthusiasm.

Part One

Introduction

1
Strengthening the Capacity of Southern NGOs

1.1 INTRODUCTION

A rapidly growing proportion of overseas aid resources is now flowing through indigenous NGOs in Africa, Asia and Latin America. Throughout the past two decades, many development agencies based in Europe and the U.S. have gradually moved away from the direct operation and implementation of overseas programmes and are working in partnership with local NGOs. Similar shifts have been occurring more recently in the funding patterns of official donors. Southern NGOs, once marginalised by official donors, are now perceived as viable local partners that offer many comparative advantages over traditional government-to-government channels of aid distribution.

Partly in response to the increasing availability of donor funding, there has been a rapid proliferation of NGOs in developing countries. While many of these indigenous agencies have the dedication, local knowledge and basic skills to engage in development work, concerns remain about the organisational capacity and long-term viability of these agencies. Northern NGOs supporting local partners find that even after providing financial support and technical advice, some Southern NGOs still fail to flourish. This is because many of the difficulties the agencies face are not due to a lack of technical skills or poorly designed delivery systems, but reflect underlying organisational weaknesses and management constraints.

Concerns about the performance and capacity of Southern NGOs are leading Northern NGOs and official donors to seek ways of strengthening their partners that extend beyond pure financial and technical support. Technical and financial inputs alone generally fail to help Southern NGOs to manage growth and change successfully, maintain clearly defined vision and purpose, and design effective strategies for achieving their objectives. Technical assistance can be vital, it is true, in making improvements in project performance. But this support does not necessarily help an NGO become more sustainable and viable in the long term. An essential element in promoting sustainable development overseas, therefore, will be assistance models which strengthen and empower local NGOs by improving their management ability and organisational capacities.

The small enterprise development sector has been the focus of much of these capacity building efforts. Many growing small enterprise development agencies in Africa – even those whose programmes are performing well – encounter problems when attempting to increase their scale. Growth creates difficult strategic dilemmas regarding the allocation of resources and the redefinition of priorities. It also raises questions regarding the suitability of existing organisational structures and procedures to manage larger programmes and increased staffing. Management problems associated with growth, therefore, are common and generally reflect pre-existing organisational weaknesses.

Successful enterprise development programmes demand a businesslike and professional approach. The pressures for performance and financial sustainability being placed on the small and micro-enterprise development sector are exceptional in their intensity. Where once donors were satisfied if the benefits of a programme were sustainable, now the service delivery mechanism itself is expected to become financially self-sustaining. The degree of financial expertise and administrative rigour now required to administer a small enterprise development programme makes it a useful sector in which to consider capacity building approaches.

This study seeks to examine the theory and practice of capacity building with reference to small enterprise development agencies in Africa. It aims to: **a)** discuss the common organisational weaknesses of small enterprise development agencies; **b)** identify and discuss approaches to capacity building and organisational development; and **c)** highlight some of the strategic implications for Northern NGOs planning to assume these roles.

Later chapters present practical case studies of interventions in Africa which illustrate different approaches to capacity building currently being implemented. These cases illustrate the common organisational challenges facing NGOs and consider the support being offered to help agencies overcome them. It is clear that organisational and institutional development need to be given a higher priority by Northern NGOs, as it is essential to consolidate viable, effective and sustainable NGO sectors in developing countries.

1.2 CORE CONCEPTS

Institutional development and capacity building have become the latest catch-phrases in the development field. In the past few years, Northern NGOs and official donors alike have begun to implement a wide variety of programmes that carry these labels. In a recent survey of Northern NGOs, over 90% of all respondents claimed to be undertaking specific approaches to strengthen their Southern partners (James 1994a). Despite the rapidly growing interest in capacity building and the growing availability of donor funds for these types of programmes, however, a common understanding of what constitutes a capacity building intervention is still lacking. Activities as diverse as core funding, the development of computer software and the provision of local staff training are now all being implemented under the banners of 'institutional development' and 'capacity building'. It is therefore important at the outset to establish what is meant by these terms and clarify basic issues surrounding these concepts (see Figure 1.1).

Capacity building
Capacity building assistance can be defined as **an explicit intervention that aims to improve an organisation's effectiveness and sustainability in relation to its mission and context** (James 1994a). Capacity building is, in fact, an umbrella word encompassing a wide range of activities that contribute to improving NGO performance and sustainability. Northern NGOs and donors implement a wide variety of capacity building approaches with a diverse range of assistance methodologies. There are, however, three main types of capacity building support that can be distinguished: technical assistance, organisational assistance and organisational development interventions. While the term capacity building is generally used to refer both to support for community-based organisations as well as that for NGOs (see, Eade and Williams 1995), this study will focus primarily on NGOs that perform an intermediary function between donors and beneficiaries

● *Technical Assistance*
Technical assistance is concerned primarily with the operational aspects of NGO performance. External inputs designed to strengthen an NGO's service delivery capacity include training, seconded staff, advisory services, and the provision of physical or technical resources. Most technical assistance inputs are designed to build a particular capacity or skill within the organisation. For example, providing an NGO with a computerised loan tracking system can improve its capacity to monitor its loan portfolio.

10

● *Organisational Assistance*

Organisational assistance inputs address organisational, rather than operational, characteristics and capacities. Management training, leadership workshops, or strategic planning consultancy, for example, can strengthen elements of an NGO's organisational capacity. These inputs are generally short-term in nature, and target a specifically defined capacity (e.g., improved administrative practices).

Most capacity building programmes have in the past focused on technical assistance inputs to bring about performance related improvements. Although the link between organisational assistance and improved project performance may be less immediate, strengthening organisational capacities can increase an NGOs efficiency and long-term viability.

● *Organisational Development Interventions*

Organisational development interventions address organisational capacities in a systematic and comprehensive way. This invariably requires in-depth and long-term engagement and may include a range of technical and organisational assistance inputs. The most common and potentially useful intervention, however, is long-term and intermittent consultancy.

The distinction between this type of support and organisational assistance is its wider, comprehensive focus on the three major areas of NGO capacity: identity and culture, management systems and structures, and programme design and technical capacity (see Figure 4.1.). The objective is to enhance an organisation's ability to manage growth and change in a planned fashion; to relate objectives to the economic, social and political environment; and to maintain clear purpose and vision.

Organisational development consultancy is meant to be facilitative, rather than problem-solving in nature. It differs from traditional management consultancy designed to perform a specific task, as it endeavours to equip the organisation itself with the wider abilities needed to deal with future problems and challenges.

Institutional Development

Although the terms institutional development and organisational development are often confused, they are not interchangeable. Institutional development is concerned with wider changes in society and seeks to initiate changes outside the boundaries of a single organisation, while organisational development is limited to the internal functioning of an organisation (Fowler *et al.* 1992:15). Institutional development is concerned with creating the conditions in which development can take place, and effecting macro-changes in the structure of social and economic relations. It can be promoted at many levels, as illustrated in Figure 1.1.

At a wider level, NGOs and donors are interested in promoting social and economic development by influencing the policy frameworks of developing countries and changing the attitudes and values of society. In order to initiate a broader process of national structural change, for example, official donors and NGOs engage in lobbying or public awareness campaigns, and encouraging reforms of public sector organisations and policies. Many NGOs in the enterprise development sector, for example, are working towards creating an enabling economic, fiscal and legal environment for small scale enterprises. In addition, some NGOs are developing linkages with the formal financial system, with the long-term objective of encouraging it to become more responsive to the interests of the marginalised sectors of society.

At a more limited level, central to the concerns of this study, is the institutional development of the NGO sector. Official donors are recognising the importance of supporting NGO networks, encouraging strategic alliances between organisations, and developing the capacity of NGO resource centres. The institutional development of the NGO sector in developing countries can provide the foundation for a more equitable and sustainable process of development.

1.3 CHANGING TRENDS IN DEVELOPMENT ASSISTANCE

The growing emphasis on capacity building and institutional development needs to be understood within the context of the rapidly evolving relationship between Northern and Southern NGOs and changing trends in development assistance. The priority assigned to the institutional development of the NGO sector in developing countries is due to a heightened awareness of the value of NGOs,which play a far greater role in development than just programme implementation. As the trend away from state-directed economic models in both the developed and developing countries advances unarrested, the reduced role of the state creates the space for private and non-governmental sectors to assume wider economic and political roles. The roles Southern NGOs play in development are not restricted to assuming service delivery functions which the state and Northern NGOs are relinquishing. They can play an important part in fostering a greater degree of social and political pluralism in developing countries.

FIGURE 1.1 Examples of Capacity Building and Institutional Development Approaches

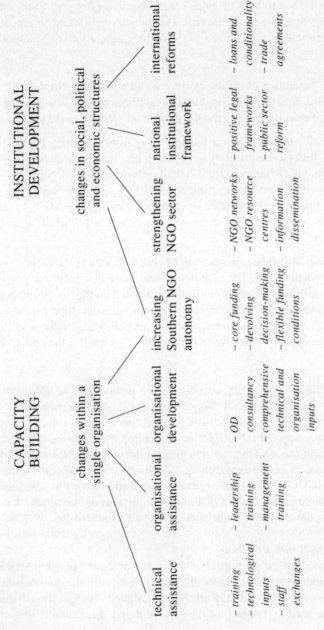

It is important to recognise that the role of Northern NGOs in development has undergone a profound transformation over the past few decades, evolving from direct welfare activities to more comprehensive efforts to change the structural factors that perpetuate poverty. This transformation can be succinctly described with reference to Korten's (1987) three generations of NGO activity:

a) The first generation of strategies were welfare oriented. Northern NGOs worked directly with communities and attempted to alleviate the conditions of poverty by transferring goods and services to the poor.

b) The second generation marked a shift away from temporary poverty alleviation strategies to attempts to initiate a process of sustainable development. NGOs promoted self-help development activities in partnership with communities. Although self-help strategies were more sustainable than previous welfare-oriented strategies, many NGOs began to recognise the need to address the wider issues of institutional development.

c) Third-generation NGO strategies are concerned with sustainable systems and institutions. These strategies recognise that even community self-help initiatives will have a limited and localised impact if the fundamental structural constraints to equitable development are not addressed. Efforts to overcome institutional or policy constraints and to create the conditions conducive to development are central to these approaches.

Capacity building strategies that contribute to the institutional development of the NGO sector are an important element of these third-generation strategies in which Northern NGOs play what is essentially an enabling role. The institutional development of the NGO sector in developing countries is a crucial element of these meso- and macro-strategies for development. Influencing the policy framework requires strengthening the advocacy skills of both Northern and Southern NGOs. It also requires networks and alliances within the sector, as well as strategic alliances with other institutions outside the sector. A supportive national development framework needs to be fostered.

Changing North-South Relations
These trends have had a clear impact on the nature of the relationship between Northern and Southern NGOs. As the division of labour in the distribution of aid gets redrawn and local NGOs are being assigned the operational roles, Northern NGOs need to rethink how they can best play this enabling role. It is

a role most Northern agencies are as yet uneasy with. Partly driven by a need for accountability to the public and to donors, they still maintain a strong preference for concrete packages of services, and shy away from less tangible methods of facilitating development that may be more difficult to justify. As Northern NGOs begin to define their role as one that creates the conditions for equitable development, then the development of sustainable indigenous institutions working towards development should become an essential part of their strategies.

The institutional development of the indigenous NGO sector contributes to a sustainable and more equitable process of economic, social and political development in a variety of ways. Channelling aid to the non-governmental sector in developing countries can help to initiate a process of decentralisation of control over resources which government-to-government aid only served to reinforce. Support for Southern NGOs can contribute, therefore, to greater local control in setting development priorities and wider participation in decision-making in resource allocation. Within the wider framework of state-society relations, the development of an independent and autonomous NGO sector (to the extent permitted by local political constraints) contributes to a greater degree of social and political pluralism in society. The emergence of a growing number of organised groups mediating between the state and society can help to curb the authoritarian tendencies of third world political systems. The proliferation of organised groups, including NGOs and community-based organisations, can enhance participation in decision-making, by mobilising and organising the population and increasing their ability to act collectively and make demands on the state and policymakers.

A thriving and mature NGO sector in developing countries will not only act as important catalyst of self-reliant development activities, but can also become a permanent sector in society that influences policy, empowers grassroots organisations, forges links with public and private sector institutions, and influences public debates. It can become a permanent sector in society actively striving to create the conditions conducive to more equitable forms of development.

Where does this leave Northern NGOs in future? As they begin to fund Southern NGOs rather than implementing projects, NGO field offices will need to play supportive roles for their Southern partners. The skills and capacities needed in the field offices must therefore reflect these changing functions. In order to respond adequately to these trends, Northern NGOs must begin to take their capacity building and institutional development roles seriously and value the contribution to development that this approach makes.

Most Northern NGOs get involved with capacity building in response to perceived weaknesses in the performance of their partners. Improved performance is the most immediate and tangible outcome of an effective capacity building programme. Yet, building the capacity of an individual organisation in isolation is ultimately going to have a limited effect if the wider institutional framework is not considered. Efforts to build the capacity of individual NGOs need to be supplemented by activities which contribute to the institutional development of the sector as a whole.

1.4 CONCLUSIONS

NGOs have long been interested in developing the capacity of organisations in Africa. Growing enthusiasm for capacity building in recent years, however, is due to changes in the content and form of support. This chapter has shown that current capacity building differs from previous NGO strategies in four key ways:

First, there has been a clear move away from uncoordinated and largely training-based efforts to systematic programmes to build organisational capacity in a more comprehensive manner. Second, more NGOs are recognising the importance of increasing the capacity of local intermediaries, rather than working directly with grassroots organisations. Third, emphasis is shifting from technical 'product' delivery-related issues to organisational 'process' capacities (Brews 1994). Fourth, although concern with existing performance is the driving factor, most Northern NGOs also seek to contribute to the institutional development of the sector.

Capacity building and institutional development have therefore become issues of central concern for Northern NGOs and are likely to increase in importance over the next few years. Several factors have caused these issues to attain greater prominence on the development agenda:

First, there are persuasive functional arguments for capacity building. Capacity building programmes can significantly improve the performance and impact of Southern NGOs. These interventions can increase the absorptive capacity of NGOs, and help them become more efficient and effective. For most Northern NGOs, this is the most immediate and tangible objective of these programmes.

Secondly, Southern NGOs are playing an increasingly important role in the aid system. With an increase in the direct funding of local NGOs by official donors, and the growing use of local intermediaries by Northern NGOs, Southern NGOs are attracting a significant proportion of aid funds. Many new Southern NGOs are emerging in a context of high expectations for their per-

16

formance. The institutional development of the incipient NGO sector in developing countries has therefore become a major concern.

Third, NGOs have an important role to play in civil society. Southern NGOs can be significant players in a process of democratisation and increased pluralism. Supporting the local NGO sector can promote a better balance between state and society, and encourage the development of a more participatory process of locally-led development.

Fourth, NGO strategies now emphasise partners over projects. In the small enterprise development sector, there has been a clear shift away from a narrow 'project' approach to one that emphasises the development of sustainable local institutions. It is clear that developing indigenous organisations able to provide services to the poor on a sustainable and long-term basis is more effective than a temporary NGO intervention.

Fifth, Northern NGOs are seeking to adopt an 'enabling' role.
Northern NGO strategies are changing. Rather than alleviating the symptoms of poverty through direct intervention, Northern NGOs are beginning to define their new role as creating the conditions conducive to a more just and equitable process of development. Developing genuine partnerships with Southern NGOs designed to strengthen and empower them is a key component of these strategies.

Part Two

Capacity Building for Small Enterprise Development Agencies: Key Issues

2
NGOs and Small Enterprise Development

2.1 INTRODUCTION

Capacity building is both difficult and complex. In order for capacity building interventions to be effective, they must be designed in relation to the specific challenges facing an NGO and be sensitive to the local cultural context. The discussion has thus far centred on general arguments for strengthening the NGO sector in developing countries. If capacity building strategies for small enterprise development agencies are to have a substantive impact, they need to address the organisational needs particular to enterprise development.

Small enterprise development agencies face tremendous pressures from many sources. NGOs supporting economic activities struggle to live up to donors' high expectations for financial sustainability and scale. Enterprise development programmes, moreover, are acutely sensitive to volatile economic trends and policy changes. These external pressures are further compounded by the complexities of engaging in economic activities. NGOs face the difficult challenge of balancing a complex and sometimes contradictory set of objectives that range from social welfare and poverty alleviation to economic growth and industrial restructuring.

NGO approaches to enterprise development have evolved dramatically over the past 15 years. Financial sustainability and clear market-driven programmes, once rejected by the NGO community, are now accepted as legitimate aims and objectives. This chapter discusses the evolving justifications underpinning small enterprise support and the changing methodologies used to assist entrepreneurs. These trends have considerable implications for the organisational requirements and management needs of small enterprise development agencies.

2.2 SMALL SCALE ENTERPRISES: FROM POVERTY ALLEVIATION TO NATIONAL ECONOMIC DEVELOPMENT

NGOs promote economic activities with a wide range of methodologies and approaches, for equally diverse reasons and objectives. These range from the social objectives of personal skills development and increased socio-political awareness to the economically defined goals of increasing disposable household income, creating employment, and contributing to a more equitable pattern of economic development (see Box 2.1). These social and economic goals are closely related and a combination of them are implicit objectives of most small enterprise development programmes. It is, however, important for NGOs to be clear about their primary goals and to articulate the intended impact of their programmes, as this will not only help determine the type of assistance that is most appropriate, but will also strongly influence the selection of the target group. Before looking at the enterprise development agencies themselves, its is important to review the evolving justifications for NGO involvement in the promotion of economic activities.

Contribution to Local and National Economic Development

Growing enthusiasm for small enterprise development within the donor community can be linked to a recognition of the role small enterprises can play in economic development. When the informal sector was first 'discovered' by the International Labour Organisation in the early 1970s, it was viewed purely as a temporary survival mechanism for the unemployed. Implicit in this conceptualisation was the assumption that the informal sector would gradually lose its significance if the modern industrial sector increased its capacity to absorb labour.

Current thinking views the informal sector not simply as a pressure valve for the unemployed, but as a potential engine of economic growth, able to absorb labour, meet local needs and initiate a process of industrial restructuring. The informal sector illustrates the extraordinary ability of marginalised sectors of society not only to survive, but to produce and generate employment in the midst of extremely adverse conditions. Traditional industrialisation strategies not only failed to provide a path to sustained and equitable economic growth, but may have hindered it by concentrating production and income, creating a dependence on imported intermediate and capital goods, and failing to generate sufficient employment.

Small enterprises have an important role to play in correcting these distortions (see Box 2.2). Small scale forms of production create employment, intensively utilise low cost, readily available inputs, and produce the goods and services consumed by low income groups. Because the modern industrial

BOX 2.1 Contributions of Small Enterprises to Social and Economic Development

Personal empowerment	Household poverty alleviation	Socio-political empowerment	Local community development	National economic development
– increased self confidence	– increased disposable income	– organisation to increase negotiating power vis-a-vis banks, local government, suppliers	– economic multiplier effect	– employment generation
– greater control over one's circumstances	– ability to access education, health care, housing	– increasing assets and resources controlled by women	– creation of local jobs and goods	– less import dependent production
– skills development	– improvements in standard of living			– industrial restructuring (see Box 2.2)

22

sector in Africa is unlikely to grow rapidly enough to absorb the growing labour force, the informal sector will continue to play an important role in providing incomes and employment for the foreseeable future.

Small enterprises are also vital for the economic development of local communities. Small enterprises create local positions of employment and produce the goods needed by the poor in their locality. This cuts down on disruptive and time consuming travel to distant markets and centres of employment. In many cases, small enterprises fill urgent community needs, such as garbage collection or water distribution. More significantly, small enterprises have a multiplier effect in the local economy. The spin-off effects of productive enterprises can stimulate the creation of new micro-enterprises through forward and backward linkages. Increasing the local base of production helps retain scarce resources within the community rather than being expended on the consumption of goods produced by the modern sector outside the community. The multiplier effect of enterprise promotion can thus stimulate local economic growth.

Consequently, small enterprise development is no longer viewed simply as a strategy for enhancing the disposable income of the poor, but is seen by official donors and the governments of developing countries as an integral part of economic development strategies.Small enterprise promotion offers an alternative to the modernisation approach to development, whose benefits, it was mistakenly predicted, would trickle down to the poor.

BOX 2.2 Economic Benefits of Small Enterprises

- use scarce resources effectively
- are highly labour intensive
- create jobs at low cost use low cost
- use appropriate locally available technology and inputs
- reduce power of oligopolies by increasing competition
- have low entry level investment requirements
- contribute to a more equitable distribution of property and wealth
- decentralise production
- produce goods to meet basic needs for low income market
- increase the circulation of money within a community

Small Enterprises and Social Development

Despite the economic focus of small enterprise development, NGOs support small enterprises for reasons that extend beyond the pure generation of profits. Small enterprise development has clear social benefits. Increasing the income generating capacity of small enterprises is an effective means of alleviating poverty at a household level. It enables unemployed people to develop their personal skills and confidence, and can contribute to a process of social and political empowerment. Enterprise development programmes have demonstrated that even a small amount of income can ease the financial pressure on a household and have a discernable impact on standards of living. The benefits of increased income manifest themselves in improved nutrition, health care, housing and education.

Self-employment also gives people greater control over their lives. At the individual level, enterprise development builds personal confidence and skills by stimulating self-initiative.Personal development can also be fostered by working at the group level. Self-help groups provide a source of mutual support and provide a much needed forum for entrepreneurs to come together to discuss common problems.

Encouraging entrepreneurs to organise can also have clear economic benefits and contribute to socio-political empowerment. Self-help groups enable entrepreneurs to challenge domination by moneylenders or intermediaries. Collective action often improves the subordinate position of informal sector entrepreneurs *vis-à-vis* these entities, giving them advantages that they are unable to obtain individually. For example, groups of entrepreneurs that purchase inputs in bulk can reduce their production costs. The collective organisation of entrepreneurs also impacts on socio-political structures. Informal sector entrepreneurs are often marginalised by local decision-making structures, and small business associations enable them to acquire legitimacy in representation to governments, municipalities, banks, and other entities.

Economic interventions may also be useful in addressing the unequal status of women within communities. Income generation and small enterprise development programmes help increase women's control over resources and assets. This in turn can address socio-political and cultural constraints by challenging assumptions about gender roles in the public and private spheres, developing management and leadership skills amongst women, encouraging a recognition of women's contribution to the economy and community, and raising the confidence and awareness of women (Piza Lopez and March 1991). Channeling resources and assets into the hands of women helps empower them to challenge male-dominated community structures.

2.3 NGO APPROACHES TO ENTERPRISE DEVELOPMENT

As the justifications for small enterprise development changed, so did the assistance methodologies. Early enterprise development programmes were designed within a social welfare framework which implied grants rather than loans, and favoured cooperatives forms of ownership over micro-enterprises. Most programmes offered intensive support to a few enterprises and provided them with on-going subsidies and advice. As the limitations of these traditional strategies of enterprise promotion gradually became apparent, some practitioners began to advocate 'minimalist' approaches based on the provision of credit to micro-enterprises. Debates then raged over the suitability of charging interest rates to the poor, and whether support for individual 'capitalist' enterprises was compatible with the social development objectives of NGOs.

The parameters of the debate have since changed. The belief that credit programmes should strive to achieve financial self-sufficiency is widespread and it is now believed that charging interest is not only possible but appropriate. The so-called 'minimalist' approach called into question the effectiveness and efficiency of NGO small enterprise work, and forced the sector to assess the cost-benefit ratio of existing strategies. Advocates of the minimalist approach pointed out that enterprises must adapt to the challenges of the market, and suggested that subsidies are potentially damaging to the sustainability of assisted enterprises (Harper 1984).

Arguing that 'credit is all you need', minimalism sparked a movement towards greater professionalism in enterprise development strategies. Most programmes now offer small scale loans in place of grants and defaulters are often vigorously pursued. NGOs have also become more selective in their targeting, acknowledging that not all potential beneficiaries have the skills and individual initiative necessary for successful entrepreneurship. More importantly, the minimalist approach, based on the provision of credit, offers a cost-effective model that can enable programmes to become financially sustainable.

Recent experiences of enterprise development programmes in Latin America, Asia and Africa are indicating that financial self-sufficiency of credit programmes is not an entirely unrealistic aspiration. Credit programmes targeted at the poor have demonstrated that commercial interest rates and/or administrative charges can be levied without affecting what have been, on the whole, impressive repayment records. Increasing numbers of credit programmes are now able to recover operating costs and meet administrative overheads.

The trend towards credit based programmes has been further stimulated by the recognition that in order to have an appreciable impact on the incomes of the poor in developing countries NGOs must develop models of assistance that enable them to reach vastly greater numbers of people. With a few notable exceptions, such as the much-lauded Grameen Bank in Bangladesh, most micro-enterprise programmes have fared poorly in terms of scale, generally reaching only a few hundred or thousand beneficiaries. The traditional, subsidised, integrated micro-enterprise project approach therefore is gradually being rejected in favour of the large-scale provision of credit at commercial rates of interest.

This steady trend towards a more businesslike and cost-effective promotion of micro- and small enterprises is based not only on a desire to increase the scale of credit programmes, but to establish financially sustainable local institutions able to become permanent sources of credit and services to the informal sector. These programmes signal a gradual departure from the 'project' approach to enterprise assistance, to one which prioritises the development of sustainable and viable local enterprise development agencies in the South. It is clear that in order to have a sustainable impact, local organisations are needed to deliver credit or other services in-country on a larger scale and on an on-going basis. Strong local organisations will have far greater impact than a temporary intervention by a Northern NGO.

Although NGOs may support small and micro-enterprises for different purposes, a clearly articulated set of objectives is essential (Hurley 1990). An agency's mission, whether immediate poverty alleviation or local economic development, will influence the definition of the target group and the choice of assistance methodology. NGO programmes vary in the degree to which they have adopted the principles of the minimalist approach. This not only strongly conditions their programme design, but has considerable organisational implications.

It is useful to conceptualise micro-enterprise promotion programmes as falling on a spectrum between two types of programmes: income generation and small enterprise development (see Table 2.1) These are two idealised types, and in practice most programmes fall somewhere in between.

Income Generation Programmes

Income generation programmes aim to enhance household income for immediate poverty alleviation and to increase the standard of living of the beneficiaries. It is the social development impact of the economic activity and increased income that is considered of primary importance, not merely the contribution of small enterprises to economic development.

Income generation programmes target the vulnerable groups in society, such as the chronically underemployed or unemployed in urban areas, and subsistence farmers or landless in rural areas. These interventions aim to provide beneficiaries with a supplementary source of income by encouraging them to develop part-time economic activities. There is little distinction between household income and business income in economic activities at this level. Profits are usually consumed immediately, with substantial reinvestment for growth in the business remaining a secondary concern.

Income generation programmes are usually directly concerned with personal empowerment and group formation, and NGOs often work in partnership with community-based organisations or encourage the formation of cooperatives. In contrast to the minimalist 'credit only' approach, these programmes provide intensive services to these economic activities, usually combining financial support, training and on-going advisory services. Income generation programmes provide these services on a heavily subsidised basis and do not usually strive to become financially sustainable.

Small Enterprise Development

Small enterprise development programmes also aim to alleviate poverty and address inequalities, but seek to do so by increasing the accumulating capacity of micro-enterprises. They attempt to stimulate local economic development and generate local jobs. To achieve these goals, most NGOs become selective in their targeting, focusing not on the most vulnerable social groups, but offering assistance to enterprises with potential for growth. For these reasons, small enterprise development programmes tend to focus on existing micro-enterprises that could be consolidated or expanded by access to credit. These programmes provide services on a cost recovery basis and aim for financial sustainability by providing credit at commercial rates of interest. Many of these programmes, therefore, conduct only limited monitoring of the impact of loans on beneficiaries' enterprises, and instead measure repayment rates, cost recovery ratios, rate of portfolio turnover, and numbers of loans disbursed.

It should be emphasised that this basic typology represents two ends of a spectrum. Small enterprise development programmes can and do achieve clear social development goals, and conversely, income generation programmes can be economically successful. Cost effective and professional methodologies can and should be applied to income generation programmes that target vulnerable groups and support supplementary sources of income. The key point is that NGOs must be clear about their objectives, and not allow social goals to detract from good economic planning.

As this brief discussion illustrates, a programme's strategic direction helps determine programme content (see Table 2.1). Small enterprise development requires a professional and market-driven, and places great demands on organisational capacity. It requires not only streamlined and rigorous systems and

27

TABLE 2.1 Characteristics of Income Generation and Small Enterprise Development Programmes

	Income Generation	Small Enterprise Development
Programme Objectives	1) enhance household income for immediate poverty alleviation 2) provide supplementary income or consolidate existing precarious economic activities 3) achieve social objectives, such as group formation	1) encourage accumulation 2) generate employment 3) stimulate local economic development 4) deliver services on cost recovery basis
Target Enterprise Character-istics	1) part-time, often intermittent 2) profits consumed immediately 3) semi-subsistence levels of production 4) no distinction between enterprise and family income 5) not sole source of family income	1) usually an entrepreneur's primary source of income 2) full time or nearly full time activity 3) profits reinvested in business 4) stable demand, sufficient working capital to maintain levels of production 5) accumulating or potential for accumulation 6) off-farm with value added
Target groups	1) chronically underemployed or unemployed in urban areas 2) subsistence farmers or landless in rural areas 3) priority given to women	1) usually targets existing micro-entrepreneurs 2) slightly better off poor
Assistance Method-ology	1) provide grants or micro loans 2) often encourage rotating savings and credit schemes 3) often provide training 4) often support cooperatives 5) intensively monitor beneficiaries' enterprises 6) supply-led	1) require larger loans for working capital and capital investments 2) focus on micro-enterprises, rather than cooperatives 3) target enterprises with potential for growth 4) assume a relatively dynamic local economy 5) market-driven

procedures, but also a clear mission and a businesslike culture.

2.4 SMALL ENTERPRISE DEVELOPMENT IN AFRICA

Small enterprise development is a complex and challenging development strategy to implement effectively. Enterprise development in rural Africa, in particular, has had a chequered history, with some successes, but also many disappointments. Its success is not only dependent on the internal organisational capacity of the implementing agency, but is also subject to external social and economic variables. Many questions have been raised about the applicability of enterprise development methodologies developed in Asia or Latin America to the unique social, economic and political environment of Africa. To be effective, intervening agencies need to have a basic understanding of the economic conditions that have constrained the emergence of a strong off-farm sector in rural areas. This section briefly highlights key constraints to enterprise development in the African context.

1) The rural off-farm small enterprise sector has been historically weak in most parts of Africa. While in countries such as India and Bangladesh there is a core sector of fledgling rural enterprises that can be assisted and expanded, in much of rural Africa there is a weak micro-enterprise base. Many historical factors have contributed to the differences between Africa and other regions. A lower level of landlessness in many parts of Africa, for example, results in fewer push factors towards non-agricultural forms of employment and self-employment (Saith 1992). Lower population densities and agricultural productivity, moreover, reduces the purchasing power of the population.

NGOs must be aware, therefore, that many rural areas are characterised by subsistence production. Limited local cash surplus creates limited local demand for off-farm industrial goods. Thus, assistance models that have been developed in the relatively dynamic urban informal sector in Latin America are unlikely to be as effective.

2) Mono-agricultural production in many regions of Africa limits the opportunities for spin-off enterprises in the areas of agro-processing or agricultural inputs. In contrast, the diversified agricultural base in Asia creates a demand for easy-entry enterprises related to agricultural production (Saith 1992).

Population density and integration between communities is also a determinant of local demand and ease of trade. Highly dispersed populations not only make NGO interventions more difficult, but act as a constraint on small enterprise opportunities. The existence of infrastructure is therefore vital in rural areas. Transport costs are often too high to make trade with urban communities or other rural areas viable for some products. Poor roads and transport services also take their toll on small enterprises by making access to raw materials and capital goods difficult.

3) One of the characteristics of small enterprises for which they are often exalted is their high labour to capital ratio, which makes them a great creator of employment for the urban and rural poor. It is less often pointed out that this comes largely at the expense of productivity. Limited access to capital goods is a major constraint to the development of productive enterprises. The limited use of power-driven tools outside urban areas and a reliance on outdated equipment leads to poor efficiency and low productivity (Nowak 1989, Siddle and Swindell 1990).

4) Government policy is generally negative or indifferent to small scale enterprises. Restrictive policy frameworks discriminate against small enterprises in many countries by introducing policy biases in favour of large scale production (Helmsing and Kolstee 1994). The recent implementation of structural adjustment programmes in many African countries has increased economic uncertainty and volatility. It is difficult to generalise about the impact of structural adjustment on small scale enterprises as this economic transformation both introduces new opportunities and imposes additional constraints. Although a sharp contraction in consumer demand in many countries affects the small scale enterprise sector, for example, trade liberalisation and deregulation increases the availability of previously scarce inputs and supplies. The elimination of price controls has led to soaring prices, but this in turn has given the low cost goods sold in the informal sector a competitive advantage. On the negative side, however, the flood of imports of consumer goods has had a severe impact on some sectors, such as the textile industry.

Small enterprise development is important in this new economic reality. Promoting small enterprises offers an alternative to an economic development model based on large formal enterprises, often foreign owned, and a dominant central state. Enterprise development encourages a process of decentralisation of control over productive resources and assets.

5) The impact of traditional patterns of social organisation on economic activities needs also to be recognised. A strong tradition of common ownership has limited experience of personal accumulation or individual entrepreneurship. Kinship networks and systems of social obligation mean that many transactions of labour, property and resources are not market-related. For example, entrepreneurs often count on kin to help them establish an enterprise, then later find themselves in the position of having to spend profits on meeting their resulting social obligations (Berry 1986).

6) Constraints also exist at the level of the NGO sector. The emergence of NGOs in Africa is relatively recent in comparison to that of Asia and Latin America. Enabling NGOs in Africa to become stronger, more effective and autonomous is vital, as the sector is poorly institutionalised and externally dependent (Fowler *et al.* 1992). Specialist enterprise development NGOs are as yet few, and many continue to operate within a welfare framework. A limited reservoir of commercial knowledge and experience available makes recruitment and staffing particulary difficult for small enterprise development agencies.

These external factors combine to increase the difficulty and complexity of implementing small enterprise development programmes in Africa. Efforts to improve the policy environment for small enterprises have therefore become an important component of institutional development strategies of NGOs and donors. An enabling economic framework and a supportive institutional environment can be promoted by direct lobbying activities, support for local small business associations and other local advocate groups, and by forging links with existing public sector and commercial institutions.

NGOs can scale-up their impact by lobbying or advising governments on the development of positive economic frameworks and legislation governing small businesses. Eliminating the constraints imposed by restrictive tax laws or import licensing, for example, can increase the competitiveness and profitability of small scale enterprises.

In 1991, APT Design and Development, a British NGO, for example, undertook a consultancy for the Ugandan Ministry of Finance and Economic Planning designed to review and assess economic policies as they affect small enterprises. As a result of the review, recommendations were forwarded by the Ministry for consideration by the Ugandan Treasury. This consultancy provided an important opportunity for an NGO to influence government policy and act as advocates for the small enterprise sector.

NGOs can also strengthen the capacity of local organisations engaged in advocacy. Southern NGOs and small business associations often lobby on macro-policy issues; but also negotiate directly with local governments and municipalities on specific issues, such as the designation of industrial estate sites, or the prevention of harassment of traders.

In addition, existing institutions in the public and commercial sectors need to be encouraged to become more responsive to the needs of small enterprises. Developing linkages with formal sector financial institutions, for example,

31

enables informal sector businessmen to access funds to which they have previously been denied. Guarantee funds offered by NGOs can be used as leverage in local banks for loans to an NGO's entrepreneur clients (Levitsky 1993). This also can instigate a process of education for local bankers by demonstrating the credit-worthiness of small enterprises. Institutional linkages that develop constructive relations with formal service providers, and encourage more participatory and inclusive policies are important for sustainable enterprise development.

2.5 CONCLUSIONS: CHALLENGES FACING SMALL ENTERPRISE DEVELOPMENT AGENCIES

It is difficult to generalise about the organisational challenges facing enterprise promotion agencies, as the range of activities within the sector makes it among the most complex within the NGO community. At the income generation end of the scale, some NGOs are assisting community-based organisations to develop small scale economic activities, while at the other end of the spectrum, some are forging links with the financial system and becoming involved in formal financial intermediation. At both ends of the scale, however, enterprise development agencies face the dual challenges of increasing their programme scale and improving the cost effectiveness of services.

Shifting towards financially sustainable methods of small enterprise promotion can be very demanding for NGOs. Often, the organisational requirements of this transition exceed an NGO's existing capacity. Problems that commonly emerge relate not only to the complex financial requirements of operating an enterprise development programme, but also to vital issues of identity and strategic orientation. This chapter has argued that because of these challenges, the need for capacity building programmes is particularly acute for the enterprise development sector. The central challenges facing these agencies include the following:

First, NGOs operating small enterprise development must abandon their grant mentality and become market-oriented. Small enterprise development agencies must develop a businesslike culture. Effective enterprise development requires a clear identity and an acceptance of economic development as an appropriate NGO activity. NGO staff from social development backgrounds often find it difficult to justify promoting individual accumulation, and these tensions can prove divisive within an organisation. It is important that staff understand the link between economic growth and social development and share the agency's vision and purpose.

32

Second, aspirations of self-sufficiency compel agencies to recover costs through service or interest charges. NGOs must undergo a fundamental change, from being supply-driven to demand-led. Agencies seeking to become financially sustainable must sell their services to their clients. In doing so, they cease to be mere donor-beneficiary intermediaries and become tied to the market. They must be aware of the real costs per client and must learn to establish realistic interest rates or service charges.

Third, the distribution of credit, which continues to comprise the core of most assistance programmes, entails complex financial and administrative functions. Managing a credit fund requires a high level of financial management skills, and stringent internal systems and accounting procedures. A lending operation requires clear systems and procedures in such areas as application assessments, loan tracking, portfolio management, and financial accounting (see Edgcomb and Cawley 1993). The degree of financial rigour required is exceptional among NGOs; not only are funds incoming from donors, but repayments incoming from beneficiaries as well.

Fourth, enterprise development agencies also have an urgent need to understand and adapt to the external operating environment. Small business programmes are directly and immediately affected by economic trends and macro-economic policies. Enterprise development agencies must develop the skills to understand and respond to the local economic context in a way most NGOs are shielded from.

Fifth, enterprise development agencies require skilled financial managers and competent business counsellors. All of these factors described above underscore the importance of staff development and recruitment to ensure an adequate and appropriate level of staff capacity. Unfortunately, it is often difficult to retain experienced managers within the NGO sector. The lure of higher paying jobs for skilled financial managers in the commercial sector makes recruitment difficult in developing countries.

A variety of organisations are involved in small enterprise development, not all are intermediary NGOs. The next chapter will consider the types of organisations involved in small enterprise development in developing countries.

3

Small Enterprise Development Agencies: Roles, Functions and Characteristics

3.1 INTRODUCTION

The institutional development of the small enterprise sector requires not only the development of NGOs, training centres, and credit agencies, but also small business associations, credit unions, and NGO support institutions. Supporting individual organisations in isolation will have limited impact in the long term, unless effective support systems for micro- and small enterprises in developing countries are established. The small-scale enterprise sector is extremely heterogeneous in composition. Enterprises have a wide range of technical and financial needs, both within and between the micro- and small enterprise sectors. A variety of support organisations that provide different but complementary services to meet these varied needs, therefore, need to be encouraged and strengthened. Institutional linkages and strategic alliances also need to be forged in order to initiate constructive relationships amongst the service providers as well as with the formal sector. Close working relationships with the financial system, business schools, and the government, signal an effective and mature enterprise support network.

Northern NGOs work with a variety of local partners that promote small-scale enterprises. This chapter will briefly describe types of local enterprise development agencies and will highlight some of their probable comparative advantages and disadvantages in service delivery. The discussion focuses on intermediary organisations that provide support services to individual or cooperatively-owned enterprises. Thus, while production cooperatives are excluded from this categorisation, community-based organisations which operate credit funds or provide other business support services to their individual member enterprises are included.

The primary organisations supported by Northern NGOs include:

1) *Community-Based Organisations (CBOs)* – operate rotating credit funds or service cooperatives
2) *Small Business Associations* – engage in both advocacy and service provision
3) *Generalist NGOs* – may contain an enterprise development component as part of a wider programme
4) *Specialist Small Enterprise Development NGOs* – provide either a comprehensive package of services or specialise in credit, training, or appropriate technology
5) *Credit Agency* – provide credit and strive for financial self-sufficiency.

This list is not exhaustive. A variety of organisations exist in developing countries that directly or indirectly can improve the availability and quality of assistance to small businesses. For example, municipalities, local government, business schools and credit unions interact with the small enterprise sector. In a more indirect fashion, NGO networks and NGO resource and training centres which act to strengthen the service providers also play essential roles.

3.2 COMMUNITY-BASED ORGANISATIONS IN ENTERPRISE DEVELOPMENT

Using community-based organisations (CBOs) as intermediaries in small-scale credit programmes is an attractive option for many NGOs. In addition to the expected economic benefits to borrowers, collaborating with CBOs enhances grassroots participation in development activities and encourages a process of socio-political empowerment of the poor. Such an approach to micro-enterprise promotion is consistent with NGOs' broad vision of social development and is compatible with their desire to develop democratic and participative programmes on the ground. At this level, therefore, there is a definite interface between economic development, immediate poverty alleviation, and community development, which may be less clear in other types of programmes.

CBOs offer some comparative advantages over other local partners for the development of small-scale credit funds for the poor as listed in Table 3.1. Traditional CBOs have their roots in the local community and are in touch with local needs and priorities. This feature makes them useful channels for operational agencies by providing a structure through which they can access the local community and reach their intended beneficiaries.

Because loan management committees of CBOs are part of the community they serve, moreover, they have knowledge of the local market and familiarity with prospective borrowers, thus facilitating loan assessment. They often also possess the unique advantage of having personal insight into an applicant's trustworthiness and character. These character assessments are important complements to the use of purely economic criteria in deciding who should receive loans. Peer pressure associated with community-based groups is also useful for ensuring repayment.

CBOs are also useful mechanisms for the mobilisation of local resources and savings. Rotating savings and credit associations, known as ROSCAs, are based on pooled, communal savings, which are then passed on to the members in turn. NGOs can channel this ability to mobilise savings and build on their own contributions to community loan funds.

Yet encouraging CBOs to become agents for economic development is not entirely without problems. The most obvious question relates to the managerial and administrative capacities of grassroots organisations. The transition from the provision of services to the management of sustainable credit systems is a challenging one for any organisation. Credit administration is an activity which demands administrative skills and rigorous procedures in order for it to be viable in the long term. This raises the question of whether an organisation designed for non-productive purposes can make the transition to managing financial activities, particularly when the skills and business-like ethos needed to make these services sustainable are generally lacking.

A more fundamental issue to consider is the impact of external intervention on the local CBO in question. Arguments for the obvious inherent "good" in strengthening community-based organisations are persuasive and often lead agencies to direct insufficient attention to some of the potential dangers of intervening in a local organisation. For example, the impact of introducing monetary resources into an organisation which has no previous experience in managing or allocating such resources can prove divisive. The sudden acquisition of capital by an organisation with few, if any, assets can introduce new forms of conflict by generating internal struggles for control over these resources. In the absence of firmly established decision-making structures, these struggles may act to undermine or even destroy the CBO.

Conflict over the control of resources is only one of the potential problems of this approach. When planning economic activities in collaboration with CBOs, an important consideration is the impact the intervention may have on the organisation's self-defined role and function within the community. Many CBOs with specific and limited functions are being encouraged to develop rotating credit systems. There is the danger that encouraging an existing CBO to take on additional activities will detract from its primary functions and objectives. NGOs need to make careful distinctions between types of CBOs before encouraging them to engage in economic activities. A further question is whether the distribution of credit is an activity compatible with the more socially-oriented or service-oriented objectives of the CBO. This is not to suggest that credit is not an appropriate activity, but rather that this may redirect the CBO's efforts away from the activities for which it was established. Time and effort dedicated to establishing the credit system will mean time and effort taken away from other activities. As with any intervention, the potential benefits must be weighed against possible adverse impacts.

The limited financial management capacity of most community-based groups indicates that they have a restricted, but important, role to play in small enterprise development. They often require on-going support and top-up grants for long-term financial sustainability. Experience to date indicates that community-based organisations are limited to micro-loans and income generation, and are generally unable to provide the levels of capital needed for small enterprise development (see Table 3.1).

Although the capacities which community-based organisations need to operate credit funds are in principle similar to those required by NGOs, the methodology of engaging with community groups differs widely from that appropriate for intermediary NGOs. An extensive literature that examines strategies for building the capacities of grassroots organisations now exists (Esman and Uphoff 1984, Uphoff 1986, Eade and Williams 1995). For this reason, this study will focus primarily on interventions targeted at small business associations and local NGOs, which have not as yet been adequately researched and addressed.

3.3 SMALL BUSINESS ASSOCIATIONS: ADVOCATES OR SERVICE PROVIDERS?

NGOs are increasingly recognising the potentially powerful role that small business associations can play in the promotion of small and micro-enterprises. Small business associations have many characteristics which place them at a comparative advantage over many other service providers to the enterprise sector. Being comprised of entrepreneurs themselves, they have a deeper understanding of the needs of the member businesses and an awareness of the impact of government policies on the sector. These organisations are well placed to provide timely, appropriate, and demand-driven services to their members.

Small business associations vary in terms of membership, which can be defined by trade, size of enterprise, or locality (Gibson and Havers 1994).

TABLE 3.1 Partners for Local Credit Distribution: Some Advantages and Disadvantages

Partner	Advantages	Disadvantages
Community Based Organisations	1) transfers skills to the poor 2) empowers grassroots organisations 3) can mobilise savings 4) derives efficiency from rapidly rotating funds 5) entails simple financial management systems 6) uses peer pressure for repayment 7) requires only small amounts of capital 8) reaches the very poor	1) capacity limited to micro-loans and income generation rather than small enterprise development 2) weak financial management skills 3) unable to manage surplus savings 4) can be distracted from their original purpose and objectives 5) may require top-up grants for long term financial sustainability
Local Generalist NGO	1) able to target vulnerable sectors of community 2) can develop strategic alliances with other service providers 3) may have long standing relationship with communities	1) local NGOs have variable capacities and may lack financial skills 2) may be perceived by community as a 'soft touch' 3) credit activities may be donor driven
Local Credit NGO	1) clear focus and mission 2) likely to recruit skilled financial managers 3) efficiency derived from scale 4) cost-effective and potentially financially stable 5) builds local institutional capacity for credit distribution 6) better prospects of client graduation to banks (via loan guarantees or letters of recommendation)	1) may not reach poorest 2) usually legally prohibited from holding savings 3) entails complex financial management 4) requires considerable human and capital investment
Direct Delivery by Northern NGO	1) clear option in places where local structures are lacking 2) full accountable staff and procedures 3) easier to monitor and adapt programme if necessary	1) long-term sustainability questionable 2) bypasses local NGOs and may inadvertantly limit local capacity to implement credit schemes 3) not integrated with local community

These range from local self-help groups of twenty or thirty entrepreneurs in the same neighbourhood, to small business associations on a national scale, with regional offices throughout. While these organisations vary in their objectives and in the services they provide, their exclusive focus on small business needs makes them a potentially effective service provider. The most effective organisations, experience has shown, are those that are clearly focused and task specific (Carroll 1992).

Small business associations perform two essential functions. First, they can represent the small enterprise sector to policy-makers and government authorities; and second, they access services for their members from existing service providers and/or develop their own capacity to deliver services. (The probable strengths of small business associations and other organisations are listed in Table 3.2).

Advocacy for policy reform is an important element of small enterprise development strategies. In most countries in Africa, small enterprises face regulatory discrimination (Kolstee and Helmsing 1994) and in some places, informal enterprises, particularly traders, are subject to active government harassment. Many economic policies unintentionally introduce biases against small enterprises, and place them at a competitive disadvantage *vis-à-vis* larger enterprises in the formal sector.

Most small business associations arise from a need to lobby local or municipal governments, and then go on to address these wider national policy issues (Sahley 1995). Associations enable informal sector entrepreneurs to articulate their interests and make demands collectively to policy-makers through a recognised form of organisation. Through membership in a registered association, informal sector businessmen can obtain legitimate representation.

Collective action has clear advantages. Membership organisations enable entrepreneurs to gain advantages which individual entrepreneurs are unable obtain individually. One common function of associations is bulk purchases of inputs, both reducing the production costs of their members' enterprises, and providing a source of income for the association. Associations sometimes implement joint marketing schemes, through the development of trade fairs, directories, or even collective sales. In these cases, associations begin to approximate service cooperatives, by enabling individual enterprises to work collectively for specific activities.

While small business associations can be powerful advocates for the small enterprise sector, their capacities as service providers are far more variable. It is difficult for an association with poorly paid or voluntary staff to develop the technical expertise in-house to run a credit programme or training course. Although some associations do engage in the provision of these types of services with varying degrees of success, it is more feasible for business associations to access existing service providers. Associations can provide an institutional home for such services and contract in the services their members need. Existing training centres, for example, can be contracted to design and implement a series of training courses in the business or technical skills that member entrepreneurs request.

Unfortunately, many small business associations suffer from serious organisational weaknesses. Many of these relate to the difficulties inherent in establishing and maintaining a fully functioning membership organisation. Sustaining a clear purpose and identity is a common problem. Small business associations often find themselves subject to intense pressures to provide concrete and tangible services, such as training or credit, and are increasingly asked by members to increase the range of services that they provide. In order to gain members and increase their income, associations which were originally set up to engage in advocacy become compelled to concentrate resources on service provision. These pressures often lead small business associations to engage in activities which they lack the capacity to implement effectively.

Membership organisations face not only financial pressures, but also face the challenge of maintaining their legitimacy within their constituent group. They need to ensure democratic functioning, good communication with members and an equitable distribution of benefits. Legitimate, dynamic and effective leaders and managers are essential; but unfortunately limited income from membership fees is often insufficient to cover the costs of staff and administration.

Despite the many challenges facing associations, they have been proven to provide effective and important services to enterprises in developing countries. A primary strength is their ability to act efficiently as a channel of service provision to individual small businesses. Most importantly, support for small business associations is an effective way to involve micro-entrepreneurs in their own development and encourage participative forms of enterprise development.

3.4 GENERALIST NGOS: EFFECTIVE ENTERPRISE DEVELOPMENT AGENCIES?

As small enterprise development gained importance on the development agenda, many generalist NGOs involved in other development activities began to establish income generation or small enterprise development programmes. As many NGOs discovered, however, the incorporation of an enterprise development component into a wider programme can be a process fraught with tensions. Generalist agencies and their staff from social development backgrounds generally find it difficult to reconcile the concern with business and profits inherent in small enterprise development with their social objectives. Intra-agency conflict between those staff opposed to small enterprise development and the specialist staff brought in to develop the programme can be intense.

There is a danger that unclear and confused objectives will result from an agency's wariness to adopt a businesslike attitude to economic interventions. This is usually demonstrated by assumptions regarding the poor's inability to pay interest on loans, or more commonly, in ideologically-driven emphasis on group forms of production, which may not reflect the preference of the poor. Inappropriate methodologies will not only contribute to poor programme performance, but may create the more significant organisational problems of a loss of focus leading to unclear purpose and strategy.

Generalist NGOs wishing to embark on the small enterprise development path should do so only if they are willing to develop the hard economic skills needed to operate an effective enterprise promotion programme. If the primary goal of an economic intervention is to enable the beneficiaries to increase their income, then NGOs must select the methods most suited to achieving these aims. This can imply considerable restructuring of organisational objectives, changes in ways of relating to the client group, rigorous financial policies, and a recomposition of staff profile.

Generalist NGOs can and do implement successful and effective small enterprise development programmes. Northern NGOs supporting Southern generalist partners, however, must be aware of the potential organisational difficulties arising from this type of work, and must be willing to support their partners through a process of strategic reformulation and planning if necessary.

3.5 SPECIALIST ENTERPRISE DEVELOPMENT NGOs

Organisations with an exclusive focus on enterprise development can include training organisations, such as the Triple Trust Organisation, South Africa; credit agencies such as the Zambuko Trust, Zimbabwe; appropriate technology organisations, such as APROTEC, Kenya, and integrated enterprise development programmes offering a range of services, such as Tototo Home Industries, Kenya. Specialist enterprise development agencies are less prone to the common pitfalls facing generalist NGOs. They are likely to attract staff with commercial experience and basic business management skills, and the specialist nature of their work means that their mission and identity is less subject to debate and confusion.

Specialist credit organisations demonstrate many comparative advantages over other local partners (see Table 3.1). Their exclusive focus on the small enterprise sector means that they are well placed to establish constructive and strategic linkages with other organisations which may have something to offer micro-enterprises. Linkages with the formal financial system, or with local management schools can be developed by such organisations.

3.6 CREDIT AGENCIES: CAN THEY BE EXTERNALLY CREATED?

In response to an absence of existing institutions capable of managing credit systems on a large scale, some NGOs and many official donors are becoming involved in attempting to establish permanent financial institutions for the poor. Underlying these programmes is the belief that specialist credit institutions are better able to develop the rigorous financial systems needed to run a viable credit programme. Efficiency demands scale, rapid turnover, effective portfolio monitoring systems and skilled financial managers. It can be suggested that compared to generalist NGOs, specialist credit institutions are more likely to be able to develop the systems needed for the large-scale delivery of credit.

Although many locally-initiated credit agencies have emerged in Africa in recent years, the predominant experience has been of donors playing a leading role in establishing new credit agencies. The sustainability of externally initiated organisations must be questioned. For those agencies wishing to build local capacity by creating local organisations, the question of genuine organisational sustainability and expatriate exit needs to be tackled at the outset. Many NGOs have found that even the best plans for gradual exit become sidetracked and postponed as a result of unresolved day-to-day management problems. It is not simply a matter of providing training or gradually transferring decision-making to local staff. The central question must be the degree of a local sense of ownership and commitment to the organisation.

Attempting to create a new organisation from the ground up is a high risk intervention. To be successful, interventions must build on existing local capacity and encourage local control early in the development of the organisations.

3.7 CONCLUSIONS

This chapter briefly examined some of the organisations that provide support

Table 3.2 Small Enterprise Development Agents: Probable Comparative Advantages in SED Promotion					
Service Providers	Credit Provision	Training	Dissemination of Information to Entrepreneurs	Institutional Linkages	Advocacy/ Policy Reform
CBO	good	poor	poor	fair	poor
NGO	good	excellent	good	good	good
Credit Institution	excellent	good	fair	good	poor
NGO Network	poor	fair	poor	excellent	excellent
Small Business Associations	poor	good	excellent	excellent	excellent
Bank	poor	poor	poor	fair	poor

services to small enterprises in the informal sector. These organisations, ranging from community-based organisations to specialist credit organisations, play different roles in enterprise development and each have their unique comparative advantages. Some preliminary conclusions can be drawn from this discussion.

First, the varied needs of the small enterprise sector cannot be met by a single organisation. A network of support organisations playing distinct but complementary roles are required for the institutional development of the small enterprise sector. Strategic alliances and linkages forged between NGOs, CBOs, management schools, banks, small business associations, and governments, can ensure the appropriate provision of services and contribute to a wider enabling environment.

Second, Northern NGOs need to select their local partners carefully, with reference to the purpose and objective of the programme. They must be sensitive to the local organisation's existing role, and be aware of the danger of encouraging them to adopt new programmes that might significantly alter their mission and purpose. This is equally relevant for NGOs as for CBOs.

Third, this discussion of the different service providers illustrates that there are no set capacity building models that can be applied to all small enterprise development agencies. Differing organisations will have different capacity building needs. Capacity building interventions need to be tailored to the specific needs and challenges facing an organisation.

Part Three

Approaches to Assessing and Strengthening the Organisational Capacity of NGOs

4

Organisational Characteristics of NGOs

4.1 INTRODUCTION

Developing sound management systems and procedures is not usually an explicit priority for most NGOs. Most of their planning efforts focus on programming and operational issues, while the important processes of organisational growth and development are rarely subject to careful and deliberate planning. NGOs continue to have a technical bias and their efforts to increase the development impact of programmes tend to focus on upgrading the technical skills of their staff or improving service delivery mechanisms. In the case of small enterprise development agencies, this may mean the development of management information systems or computerised loan tracking software. Although such technical improvements can enhance the performance of an NGO, the underlying organisational abilities to use technical, financial and human resources effectively remain untouched.

NGOs have less readily acknowledged the link between their internal organisational capacities and their programme performance in the field. Most NGOs allow their organisational capacities to develop in a spontaneous and unplanned manner, assuming that the organisational and managerial capacity to handle growth will develop as needed. In most cases, these assumptions are proved incorrect. If organisational growth and change are to be managed successfully, they need to be planned. This point is particularly relevant to young NGOs in developing countries that are simultaneously experiencing exponential growth and donor expectations of improved performance. Many small enterprise development agencies in Africa are expanding rapidly, and as a result, many are exhibiting some of the common organisational problems associated with growth.

Efforts to build the capacity of Southern NGOs will only be effective if they are based on an understanding of the management needs specific to the NGO sector. While a full discussion of the organisational characteristics of

NGOs is beyond the scope of this study, this chapter will briefly discuss some of the key elements which distinguish their management needs from those of other types of organisations.

4.2 ORGANISATIONAL CHALLENGES FACING NGOs

The management of development agencies is very complex. NGOs work in turbulent political and social contexts and are subject to a wide range of external pressures from governments, communities, and donors. In these volatile contexts, viable and effective development work must be underpinned by strong and competent organisations. Good management, clear internal structures, well defined responsibilities, and appropriate and efficient administrative systems are essential for the effective functioning of any organisation.

Effective NGOs need to develop a myriad of capacities that relate not only to management but also to identity, mission, and interpersonal relations, to mention but a few. These capacities provide the foundation that enables an NGO to use its human, technical and financial resources to their fullest potential. A more comprehensive and detailed mapping of the organisational capacities of NGOs can be found in the INTRAC organisational assessment framework (see Chapter 5).

NGO capacities can be roughly grouped under three categories. These capacities can be thought of not as separate components, but as building on each other in a multi-layered organisation (see Figure 4.1):

- **identity, culture and purpose:** Identity, culture and purpose are at the heart of an NGO's capacity. These include such factors as a clear ideology of development and sense of purpose; in addition to cultural aspects of the organisation, such as good interpersonal relationships, effective conflict resolution mechanisms and positive staff-management relations. Organisational development interventions begin by addressing these core characteristics (see Figure 4.1.). A clear identity forms the essence of an effective NGO.

- **management systems and structures:** NGOs also require effective management systems and structures. These procedural capacities include such skills as effective decision making, clearly defined roles and responsibilities, and effective financial management. Poor NGO management manifests itself in poor programme performance. The internal operations of an NGO need to function smoothly in order for it to intervene successfully in communities.

47

- **programme and technical capacity:** The programme and intervention strategies are the external and most visible capacities of an NGO. This includes the organisation's technical capacity to deliver services, as well as to develop an effective and appropriate strategy based on a thorough understanding of the local economic, social and political context. Clearly, there is significant overlap between these capacities. An effective strategy, for example, can only be designed if the organisation has a clear and unambiguous sense of purpose.

As straightforward as these organisational characteristics may appear in theory, they can be difficult to maintain in practice. A variety of factors influence the organisational capacities of NGOs, many of which arise from the complex nature of development work and the culture of voluntary organisations and staff. Some of the problems NGOs face stem from the complexities of being non-profit and value-driven organisations. NGOs differ from commercial organisations in many fundamental ways. In order to respond appropriately to the common organisational problems that face NGOs an understanding of these differences is necessary. This section will consider the characteristics of NGOs as organisations which make their management particularly challenging.

Figure 4.1 Areas of NGO Capacity

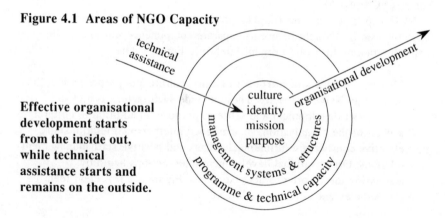

Effective organisational development starts from the inside out, while technical assistance starts and remains on the outside.

Value-Driven and Voluntary Organisational Culture
The defining characteristic of NGOs is their value-driven and voluntary nature. They make a clear distinction between themselves and the commercial and public sectors, as exemplified by the use of the terms 'non-profit' and 'non-governmental' to define themselves. This value-driven identity strongly conditions the organisational culture of NGOs. This culture is one that priori-

tises strategic programme planning over organisational development plans. It is in part the intensive focus on output that leads NGOs to overlook the importance of their own internal management. Focusing intensively on management is feared to take away valuable time from programme activities. In their desire to develop the capacity for rapid response, NGOs allow little time for introspection and internal planning.

NGOs are also wary of adopting mainstream management models that are designed with profit maximisation as the primary objective. Most NGOs prefer to adapt (often rather haphazardly) their own management techniques, with varying degrees of success. While it is true that there is much that distinguishes NGOs from the business sector, this should not be used, as is often the case, as justification for the wholesale rejection of commercial management practices. There is much that the NGO sector can learn from the commercial sector, in particular its concern for maximising cost-effectiveness, efficiency and quality. NGOs are now recognising that being 'voluntary' need not mean being unprofessional. Developing and adapting management practices suited to the distinct reality of development NGOs needs to become a priority.

Other aspects of NGOs' value-driven, organisational culture that have practical implications for their management include staff composition, which is likely to be technically- based rather than management oriented. NGO directors and staff are more likely to be hired for their development expertise and commitment than for their management skills and experience. NGO directors and programme managers may find themselves burdened with management responsibilities for which they are unprepared, and this may contribute to poor management. Weak management and planning ability, furthermore, is also often found at the level of NGO trustees. A frequent problem throughout the voluntary sector is an ineffective and aloof board of trustees. Trustees are often chosen for their prestigious standing in the community, and are brought in on a voluntary basis. In many cases, they have limited time to dedicate to fulfilling their important supervisory roles. Despite their importance, however, trustees' performance is almost never subject to assessment or appraisal, and they are rarely targeted for training.

In a related point, the value-driven basis of NGO work tends to generate an organisational culture of deep commitment and ideological conviction. NGOs attract staff who are highly committed to a set of beliefs and this emotional commitment to an agency's work is one of the great strengths of the non-profit sector. However, this intense personal commitment often proves divisive. Ideological friction within an organisation is not uncommon, and personal agendas sometimes conflict with an organisation's remit. In addition, an emotional or overcommitted reaction to a problem facing the target community can lead an NGO to a hasty or inappropriate response.

Internal ideological disagreements can be particularly pronounced in enterprise development agencies. The social development background of most NGO staff can coexist uneasily with a strategy whose success is often defined in economic terms, such as income generated per client, cost per loan, etc. Small enterprise development agencies are likely to have staff from a social development background in addition to those with commercial skills, and this combination can create internal tensions. More significantly, this type of fundamental ideological conflict within an agency can lead to confused identity, role and strategy. A clear balance between social and economic objectives that is understood by all staff is essential if such internal conflict is to be minimised.

NGOs as Intermediaries

The intermediary function non-profit agencies perform means that they have multiple constituencies. While commercial organisations are able to attune themselves exclusively to the needs of their consumers, NGOs must attempt to satisfy demands from both donors and beneficiaries. NGOs must remain responsive to their target groups, even though they are directly affected by donor priorities and funding trends. The resulting dual accountability to both groups can create serious tensions within an organisation.

Balancing the sometimes conflicting concerns and expectations of these two key stakeholders increases the complexity of NGO management. On one hand, the virtually unlimited needs of target communities can pressure NGOs into assuming new roles for which they are poorly prepared. On the other, donor priorities sometimes lead NGOs to develop projects that are easily financed, even if they fall outside their original remit or mission (Campbell 1986). These external pressures can lead to a series of short-term modifications in project direction, which accumulate in the long term to become an unintentional change in strategic direction. Clearly articulated aims and objectives are therefore essential for an NGO to remain focused and effective.

A further problem is that NGOs lack clear, institutionalised feedback from those that use their services. NGOs are unique in that the consumers of NGO services (communities) are distinct from the purchasers (donors). Although all NGOs profess to be primarily accountable to their target groups, their intermediary role in the funding channel means that direct feedback regarding the suitability of a proposed activity, or of overall performance, is likely to come from donors. While commercial companies get automatic feedback from consumers in the form of demand, NGOs must themselves attempt to assess the impact of their services on beneficiaries.

This problem is compounded by the difficulty in evaluating qualitative NGO objectives. Commercial organisations have a clear and iron-clad bottom line by which performance is measured: profits. The objectives of agencies involved in promoting development, in contrast, are not so straightforward. NGOs face the challenging task of attempting to quantify or measure the extent to which qualitative objectives have been achieved (see Marsden *et al.* 1994).

Project Focus

Most NGO planning is done on the basis of project cycles, rather than the methodical and systematic long-term institutional planning needed for coherent and managed growth. There are, of course, genuine pressures on NGOs for short-term strategic plans, imposed by project-based donor requirements. However, this project focus has many consequences.

First, the emphasis on specific, time-bound 'projects' encourages NGOs to focus on short-term details instead of long-term horizons. A two-year project is predicated on the assumption that short-term results are achievable. Second, the project-based existence of most intermediary NGOs also encourages them to become single-minded in their concern for output. NGOs justify their existence by 'doing' rather than 'being'. However, this heightened emphasis on action often results in a flurry of activity, with limited time devoted to careful planning and necessary reflection and assessment. Long-term planning needs to be conducted both for external programme activities and internal organisational issues. Third, project funding encourages NGOs to compartmentalise their activities into distinct units, whereas wider, integrated perspectives might be more effective. These potential problems can be avoided by encouraging Southern partners to develop long-term plans that include both programme strategies and plans for organisational growth and development. This process encourages NGOs to take a step back from constant activity to reflect on and assess their performance and future direction. Progress is being made in the small enterprise development field, where projects are being replaced by ongoing credit programmes or training centres. This trend away from timebound projects to long-term assistance offered by sustainable local organisations is a positive one and should be encouraged by Northern NGOs and official donors.

The Grant Mentality

The grant-based financing of development work also has considerable implications for financial management. The grant mentality is hard to break and subsidies, once established, prove extremely difficult to withdraw. The attitudes of administrators who manage "gift" money is likely to be more lax than commercial managers with an easily discernable bottom line. If the link between financial support and measurable performance is tenuous, and grants are automatically forthcoming, incentives for strict financial management are reduced. Dependency on external sources of finance also creates planning complications as a result of the financial uncertainty generated by constantly fluctuating levels of income. NGOs need to establish diversified funding portfolios and increase the cost recovery basis of services in order to retain some autonomy from funding trends.

Need for Participatory Management Styles

NGOs with numerous projects in the field need to develop decentralised and participatory decision-making structures, in order to ensure flexibility and maintain the ability to adapt to changing circumstances. Participatory planning processes are particularly important for NGOs as closest contact with beneficiaries is had by field staff. Staff throughout the organisation need to feel that they can contribute to the development of policy and strategy.

Despite this, some NGOs in the South suffer from over-centralised, top-down structures, often caused by a strong and possessive founder. Dynamic and charismatic individuals who take the initiative to create a new agency often find it difficult to relinquish direct control and delegate responsibilities. In agencies where most key decisions are taken by an individual, the institutionalisation and decentralisation of decision-making is inhibited. Clearly defined roles that ensure that staff understand their tasks and responsibilities are essential for the smooth functioning of any organisation.

Complex Relationship with Environment

NGOs operate in turbulent political and economic environments, and the way they seek to relate to their environment differs from that of commercial organisations. Commercial organisations attempt to shield themselves from the impact of changes in the environment through defensive strategies, such as building up stocks or seeking new suppliers (Fowler 1990). Many of the variables that determine the success of a commercial venture are internally controlled, or can be predicted and avoided by careful planning. NGOs, in contrast, are forced to adapt to changing environments. The objective of most development projects is in fact to make changes in the wider social, political or economic environment. NGOs need to remain deeply embedded in the community and are therefore acutely sensitive to social or political changes.

NGOs require clear information-gathering methodologies that enable them to predict or measure changes in the target community, and adapt their programmes accordingly. The success of any intervention methodology is predicated on an thorough understanding of the problem facing the community. For small enterprise development agencies, a basic understanding of the local economy is crucial to the success of a programme.

52

BOX 4.1 Possible Causes of Poor NGO Management

- Management not a priority
- Focus on details, not horizons
- Wish to respond immediately
- Overcommitted and emotional response
- Inability to decentralise decision making

- True collaboration with other agencies rare
- Individual agendas imposed on organisational remit
- Insecure funding inhibits planning
- Grant mentality

Source: INTRAC 1994

4.3 CONCLUSIONS

There is still some debate and controversy surrounding the relevance of organisational development to the NGO sector. NGOs are understandably wary of adopting potentially inappropriate management models from the commercial sector which place a premium on profitability and efficiency, and allow little room for values or non-economic indicators of success. There is a concern, in particular, that consultants will impose Western management practices on developing countries. Yet, while the notions of ethics and social responsibility in business become more important in today's marketplace, the non-profit sector too must reconsider its performance and seek to learn what it can from the commercial sector in terms of efficiency and efficacy.

There are many characteristics of NGOs which make them unique as organisations. Many of the common problems facing NGOs, such as internal conflict, poor leadership, weak management and poor long-term planning can be traced to some of the factors highlighted in this chapter. Some of the possible causes of poor NGO management are listed in Box 4.1. Their intermediary role makes them subject to pressures from many stakeholders, and creates insecurity resulting from reliance on donor funds. Effective NGOs are aware of these potential pitfalls, and engage in long term organisational planning, in addition to strategic, programme planning. Effective organisations are those that pay attention to their internal capacities, and strive to develop clear structures, appropriate administrative systems, and strong leadership.

The recent trend towards developing NGO based management practices is a positive one. NGOs engaging in capacity building of their Southern partners can turn to the growing number of consultants specialising in NGO management issues. This chapter, rather than focusing on common management problems of NGOs, attempted to highlight some of the underlying causes of poor NGO management. Some of the more salient conclusions from this discussion are summarised below:

First, NGOs need to integrate institutional planning into their strategic planning efforts. NGOs have a tendency to focus single-mindedly on the external environment when considering long-term and strategic planning. This is a natural outgrowth of the NGO sector's aim to meet the needs of its target group, and to provide a valuable service. This focus on the target group, however, needs to be counterbalanced by an understanding of how internal organisational capacities affect the ability to achieve these objectives. NGOs tend to equate their capacity for growth as their technical ability and logistic capacity to deliver more services. The organisational elements needed for programme expansion are often overlooked. NGOs need to recognise the links between their own internal capacities and their programme performance.

Second, developing and disseminating management practices which have proven effective for NGOs should receive greater priority. Solutions to NGO management issues can only be developed on the basis of an understanding of the organisational characteristics of NGOs. There is a growing literature that considers organisational characteristics and management theory from an NGO perspective (Drucker 1990, Handy 1990). However, much of this remains academic in nature and insufficient effort is being directed to disseminating this information to Southern NGOs in a practical way.

Third, it is important to point out that the staff profile and business-oriented nature of small enterprise development agencies may make them less prone to these drawbacks. Despite the enormous external constraints and the complexity of developing economic interventions, small enterprise development agencies may have some important advantages. In sharp contrast to other NGOs, they are more likely to seek staff with good financial and administrative management skills, and with commercial experience. In addition, the desire for self-sufficiency means that they are more likely to be aware of cost-benefit ratios and be engaged in careful financial planning and forecasting. The skills held by their technical staff, who are likely to be financial managers rather than engineers or anthropologists, can be used to improve internal organisational practices. Small enterprise development agencies have the potential to manage effectively their own organisational growth and development.

5
Organisational Assessment of NGOs

5.1 INTRODUCTION

NGOs need to develop more systematic ways to assess their organisational capacities and identify their strengths and weaknesses. In order for NGOs to improve their ability to manage their human, financial and technical resources, they first need to appraise realistically their own capacities. Organisational assessment frameworks are currently being developed which provide guidelines for appraising the capacities of an organisation. Among the areas to be assessed include an NGO's mission, legitimacy in the community, degree of transparency, and management capacity.

Organisational assessment can facilitate a deeper understanding of the character of an organisation, and as such is gaining relevance for Northern NGOs, both in the selection of partners, and in the development of capacity building interventions. As Northern NGOs move from project funding to long-term partner support, they need to look beyond the technical capacity of Southern agencies and consider their underlying organisational characteristics. Despite the importance to a partnership of shared values and compatible objectives, many Northern NGOs continue to base the selection of Southern partners on the quality of the written project proposal and the perceived value of the programme. This rather cursory approach to partner assessment is understandable given the lack of resources and time available to Northern NGOs, and their traditional "project" focus.

Partnership, however, entails more than the transfer of funds. In order to develop a long-term relationship based on common understanding, shared values, and mutual learning, Northern NGOs need to assess more than just technical capacity. Are potential or existing partners clear in their objectives and mission? Do they have legitimacy within the communities in which they work? Is the organisation able to adapt to evolving conditions and manage growth? These are the sorts of questions which Northern NGOs are increasingly asking.

Qualitative assessment of the strengths, weaknesses and essential character of an organisation is a complex process, and the development of organisational assessment methodologies for NGOs is still in its infancy. There is, however, a growing amount of research and attention being placed on processes of organisational assessment as an integral component of organisational development. This chapter highlights the importance of this assessment for developing effective and appropriate capacity building interventions.

5.2 ORGANISATIONAL ASSESSMENT FRAMEWORKS

A wide range of organisational capacities are essential for effective NGO performance. Organisational assessment frameworks offer a comprehensive mapping of the essential characteristics of an effective and viable NGO, and provide a basis for beginning to understand and assess these. Organisational assessment tools identify key capacities in the areas of programme performance and community intervention practices, administrative and management practices, as well as the more intangible issues of organisational culture and identity. These frameworks may be in the form of graded checklists, detailed questionnaires, or a basic outline of capacities for discussion. Organisational assessment tools are guidelines only. They are intended to provide a basis for discussion and facilitate a process of self-assessment of an organisation in relation to its stage of development, and in the context of the wider social and political environment.

Organisational assessment frameworks are currently being developed by INTRAC and others in order to improve the ability of NGOs to assess their own and their partner's organisational effectiveness. Developing simple and practical organisational assessment tools, without losing their flexibility and relevance for a wide range of NGO types, sizes and stage of development, must be a priority for NGOs seriously interested in organisational development.

These frameworks have multiple purposes. First, they can help Northern NGOs better select new partners to work with. The purpose of organisational assessment in this role is to enable the Northern NGO to look beyond the programme performance indicators, and look at other essential characteristics of an agency, such as its mission, its legitimacy in the community, and its organisational capacity. It should be stressed that the issue here is of a better understanding of the potential partner agency rather than a quantitative evaluation of its performance. However, the use of these frameworks by Northern NGOs with Southern NGOs with which they have yet to form any kind of relationship is problematic. An effective and in-depth organisational assessment process requires an open and honest relationship, and most Southern NGOs understandably are uncomfortable with the notion of revealing their weaknesses to a potential funder. In these cases, an organisational assessment framework can be used by a Northern NGO merely as a mental checklist of organisational characteristics that can be kept in mind when deciding which Southern NGOs to support.

Second, organisational assessment can play a role in selecting which existing partnerships should be deepened. Some Northern NGOs are scaling down the number of overseas partners they support and are instead developing more in-depth and substantive partnership with fewer, but like-minded Southern NGOs. In many cases, Northern NGOs maintain funding relationships with Southern NGOs for historical reasons, even though the Southern NGO may have evolved substantially in its programming and policies, and may no longer share the same values and development objectives with its donor partner. Organisational assessment can assist Northern NGOs wishing to examine and evaluate their existing partnerships and consider how they can best be taken forward.

Third, and most importantly, organisational assessment serves as an initial diagnostic stage of a capacity building programme. As Albrecht (1983) notes, 'Prescription without diagnosis is malpractice, whether in medicine or in management'. Unfortunately, this point is often overlooked by NGOs when developing capacity building strategies for their Southern partners. Organisational weaknesses are overgeneralised as 'management problems', and this often leads to generic management training or other inputs that have not been tailored to the needs of the NGO. Effective organisational development strategies can only be designed on the basis of a proper understanding of the organisational strengths and weaknesses of the NGO in question.

Fourth, Northern NGOs must recognise that they also need to assess their own organisational capacities, and seek ways to build upon them. Organisational assessment frameworks are a useful tool which can guide an NGO through a process of self-evaluation and assessment. Northern NGOs are often quick to point out the weaknesses of their implementing partners, but this view must be tempered with a critical assessment of their own organisational constraints. The strengthening of the NGO sector in the North is an equally important challenge facing the aid community.

Box 5.1 State of the Organisation[1].

NGO CAPACITIES:

- Identity
  - *Values:* an unambiguous statement of belief
  - *Vision:* a shared understanding of the future being worked toward
  - *Theory:* an understanding of cause of problem/poverty
  - *Mission:* a clear mission statement
  - *Strategy:* a long-term plan based on values, vision, theory and mission

- Legitimacy
  - *Social:* active involvement of stakeholders
  - *Legal:* statutes/constitution appropriate to the present day

- Accountability
  - *Stakeholder Satisfaction:* retain support of key stakeholders

- Community Intervention Process
  - *Determining Context:* data on situation available
  - *Target Group Selection:* criteria for selection exist
  - *Target Group Engagement:* participative methodology used
  - *Negotiation of Participation:* agreements or contracts exist
  - *Timely Delivery of Services:* agreements or contracts exist
  - *Feedback:* minutes, meetings, reports, work plans in written form
  - *Evaluation:* participant evaluation methodologies used
  - *Withdrawal:* criteria for withdrawal exist

- Structure
  - *Clear Division of Tasks:* clear job descriptions, organisational charts available

- Leadership
  - *Vision:* vision articulated
  - *Honesty:* regarded as honest and having integrity
  - *Competence:* technical and decision-making ability demonstrated
  - *Consistency:* leaders accessible and accountable with open communication

[1]Part one of the INTRAC Organisational Assessment Framework

- Policy Intervention Process
  - *Information Gathering and Analysis:* data and resource base readily accessed
  - *Policy Decision-Making Processes:* policy papers produced
  - *Formulation of Policy Alternatives:* policy alternatives available
  - *Lobbying and Advocacy:* contacts, relationships, networks forged

- Support Systems
  - *Financial:* annual budgeting occurs with key staff involvement
  - *Planning, Monitoring and Evaluation of Outputs:* targets exist, community-based evaluation conducted
  - *Management:* structures and procedures for collaboration between systems exist, alongside periodic management information reviews, and assessments of achievement against expectations
  - *Personnel:* human resource development policies, appraisal methods clearly articulated
  - *Decision-Making:* division and allocation of authority recognised
  - *Communication:* staff have access to accurate and timely information
  - *Administrative:* effective filing, effective records of information available
  - *Fund-Raising:* funding proposals, information, and strategies exist

- Culture
  - *Power:* how decisions are made
  - *Conflict Management:* procedures for conflict resolution
  - *Learning for Change:* signs of organisational adaptation
  - *Concern for Quality:* signs of increasing standards
  - *Expression of Consistency:* consistency of practices and policy
  - *Inter-staff Relations:* good relations between staff at all levels

- Resources
  - *Competent Staff:* professional qualifications, years of experience
  - *Committed Staff:* share and express values, low absenteeism
  - *Financial Stability:* fluctuations between and within sources, diversity, core costs funded, adequate plans and budgets
  - *Physical Capacity:* sufficient to implement programme

Source: INTRAC 1993

5.3 THE APPLICATION OF ORGANISATIONAL ASSESSMENT FRAMEWORKS

While a variety of frameworks illustrating various NGO capacities have been developed, methods of implementing these have yet to be fully explored. A continuum of approaches exist, ranging from an interpretative approach based on dialogue and full stakeholder participation, to a more mechanistic and quantitative approach. The organisational assessment tool provides only a basic framework that identifies the key capacities of an effective NGO, thus providing a basis for the development of appropriate indicators.

An organisational assessment framework developed by INTRAC examines a wide range of NGO abilities, grouped under three major capacity areas: the state of the organisation, its external linkages, and its programme performance. The first of these, the state of the organisation, highlights a range of internal, organisational characteristics such as culture and identity, which while an important aspect of organisational performance, are not often assessed explicitly. The key competencies identified by INTRAC in the first part of its organisational assessment framework are listed in Box 5.1.

These frameworks are effective and useful only if flexibly applied. Effective organisational assessment is best conducted by an external facilitator to lead the process in an interpretative and participative assessment way. The facilitator's role is to elicit a wide variety of views and perceptions at all level of the organisation. While there are many methods of conducting an internal assessment, the process can be roughly divided into five steps. (For a useful discussion of interpretative and participative forms of evaluion, see Marsden *et al.* 1994.)

1) The facilitator and NGO must share an understanding of the assessment process and the support of senior management must be engaged. It is essential that there is an agreement on the methodology to be used and that the NGO involved is fully committed to the process. It is important to involve personnel at all levels in the formulation of the objectives of the self-assessment process. Some staff may fear that the Northern NGO's interest in the assessment process is to find fault or exclusively to identify weaknesses, rather than as a basis for a plan for improvement. Clarity and transparency in the planning stage can minimise potential misunderstandings and lead to improved relations throughout the entire process.

2) The facilitator uses the organisational assessment framework to elicit views from staff at all levels of an organisation, from the board of trustees to managers and staff. Responses can be obtained through a combination of

one or more of the following:
- written questionnaires
- semi-structured individual interviews
- open discussions with individual staff members
- focused and facilitated group discussions

Key stakeholders must participate and be engaged in the assessment process in order to allow a comprehensive and balanced view of the organisation to emerge. Staff should be encouraged to identify the main weaknesses in the organisation and discuss the reasons for them. The information generated in this second stage can then form the basis of discussion within the organisation.

3) The facilitator reports back the more significant findings to the organisation in a feedback workshop. This workshop enables all members of the organisation to respond to some of the key issues arising from the earlier stage. It is essential that this process be transparent and open, allowing for the expression of competing views. It is at this stage, that the organisation can begin to collate responses and draw conclusions regarding the priority areas for improvement.

4) Indicators to monitor improvement are selected and developed. Once the organisation has identified the weaknesses which it wants to address, indicators must be developed in order for the NGO to monitor its improvements in this area. The qualitative nature of many of these capacities makes the selection of indicators difficult. Without precise baseline indicators, however, it will be difficult to assess the impact of subsequent capacity building efforts. The process of negotiating indicators, furthermore, is an important part of institutional learning which forces the organisation to identify concrete ways it can improve. The selection of indicators can be a creative and reflective process.

For example, the following indicators could help assess the degree to which an NGO is rooted in the local community:

a) a percentage of field staff who speak the local language, or belong to the local ethnic group
b) the dissemination of reports in an appropriate style and language to the target community, staff and government
c) minimum of three-quarters of staff time is spent working directly with the target group in the field.

While acknowledging the limitations of the indicators in providing a thorough understanding of the capacity they attempt to measure, these examples illustrate that even qualitative and intangible characteristics can be subject to some form of standardised assessment. The existence of an agreed set of indicators at the beginning of an intervention provides essential baseline information, and enables the organisation to measure its own progress and improvement.

Organisational assessment frameworks and processes for the NGO sector still need to be refined and tested in the field. However, these frameworks, even at their incipient stage, provide a useful guideline for both externally facilitated and internally initiated assessment processes. Some of the key elements of a successful organisational assessment process are summarised in Box 5.2.

Box 5.2 Important Elements of an Effective Organisational Assessment Process

- **Sense of Local Ownership and Commitment**
  The Southern NGO must perceive value in the organisational assessment and organisational development process. If imposed by Northern donors and is engaged in unwillingly, the process is unlikely to be constructive or fruitful.

- **Self-Assessment**
  Organisational assessment is essentially a facilitated process of self-assessment. The assessment process should encourage the recipient NGO to identify its own strengths and weaknesses.

- **Establishing Priorities and Setting Clear Objectives**
  The organisational assessment process should culminate in the identification of priority organisational areas for improvement.

- **Developing Indicators**
  A key element of the assessment process is the development of indicators to monitor and evaluate improvement in the organisation's effectiveness. This negotiated process of selecting indicators also provides baseline data prior to an organisational development intervention.

- **Negotiating Future Inputs**
  This diagnostic stage should lead to a negotiated identification of appropriate intervention methodologies and should provide the basis for agreement on the role of capacity building in the ongoing partnership.

5.4 CONCLUSIONS

Organisational assessment tools designed for use within the NGO community are currently being developed and improved. As Northern NGOs begin to examine more critically their partnerships with Southern implementing agencies, both agencies need to understand better each other's strengths, weaknesses, and purpose. While an assessment of the technical capacity of NGOs must remain an integral factor in the selection of a partner, it is equally important to understand the vision and culture of that organisation.

First, organisational assessment is most effective and comprehensive when performed in an interpretative and participative way. Although time consuming, this approach enables all of the key stakeholders to feel part of the process, leading to the development of a more appropriate and effective capacity building plan. Conversely, these tools are also sometimes used purely as a checklist against which NGOs can roughly attempt to appraise the comparative strengths and weaknesses of a number of Southern NGOs. While it is important to encourage Northern NGOs to consider these organisational characteristics when assessing partners or choosing between project proposals, the mechanistic use of the framework entails the real danger of misinterpretation or unsound judgements.

Second, organisational assessment should not be tied to funding or it can become a threatening process to the NGO involved. It must be stressed that organisational assessment is designed to instigate change and improvement. It is not meant to find fault or assign blame. It is hoped that this self-evaluation will be an enlightening process which culminates in the development of an appropriate plan for establishing a sounder, more professional base for effective development work.

Third, organisational assessment frameworks are relevant to Northern NGOs. Recent interest in capacity building has focused largely on strategies for supporting emerging NGOs in developing countries. Northern NGOs must first and foremost assume responsibility for their own capacity building. Organisational assessment can be a useful in-house process feeding into organisational planning sessions.

6

Capacity Building Models and Approaches

6.1 INTRODUCTION

Northern NGOs use a wide spectrum of approaches to strengthen local partner organisations, ranging from technical inputs to individual NGOs to strategies to promote the institutional development of the NGO sector as a whole. These inputs differ in their impact and the depth of change that they can induce. They also differ widely in terms of the cost incurred, and in the degree of commitment and expertise required to execute them fully and effectively.

The choice of capacity building input or combination of inputs needs to be context specific. The intervention must take into account the stage of development of the Southern organisation and its specific organisational needs as identified through a systematic process of organisational assessment. The nature of the capacity building support, moreover, must also reflect the wishes and priorities of the local partner. The process of developing a capacity building strategy should be based on open negotiation between the two parties, leading to a consensual plan of action.

Prior to examining the types of support services used to strengthen Southern NGOs, it is important to stress the purpose of capacity building interventions. Capacity building and organisational development are not ends in themselves. Improved NGO management is only important inasmuch as it improves an NGO's ability to meet the needs of the communities with which it works. Capacity building interventions seek to help NGOs become more effective by increasing their capacity to:

- manage changes in the operating environment
- manage organisational consolidation and growth
- target and use resources effectively
- assess and respond to clients' needs
- become sustainable and viable in the long term.

In sum, effective capacity building interventions improve an NGO's organisational and technical performance, enhancing its capacity to provide appropriate and sustainable services to its target groups.

In addition to specific capacity building inputs, many NGOs and official donors are designing strategies at a sectoral level designed to promote the institutional development of the NGO sector in developing countries. Strategies to strengthen individual NGOs need to be implemented alongside those which promote the local supply of support services and encourage a favourable policy framework for the NGO sector. Only if wider changes are instituted throughout society and permanent NGO resource systems are established, can a thriving and mature NGO sector emerge in developing countries.

6.2 CAPACITY BUILDING INPUTS

Capacity building does not refer to a narrowly defined range of services, but encompasses any outside intervention or input aiming to increase the organisational or technical capacity of an NGO. Outside inputs that can strengthen an NGO's performance include training, the provision of volunteers, physical and technical improvements, organisational development consultancy, and the dissemination of information. This section will briefly discuss some of the advantages and potential limitations of these approaches.

Technical and Management Training
Human resource development is the cornerstone of local capacity building. The foundation for a strong local NGO sector is the existence of a local pool of skilled and talented NGO workers. In a recent survey, training ranked as the input most often provided by Northern NGOs to their Southern implementing partners (James 1994a). Training in technical skills has long been the preferred strategy by Northern NGOs to address the relatively weak skills base in most developing countries.

This approach may be less relevant now than in the past. The availability of technically qualified and educated staff in developing countries has increased dramatically over the past decade. Where training gaps still remain, however, is in the area of management and administration. The emphasis and content of training being provided to NGO staff is only now beginning to adapt to these changing needs. Although technical training has yet to give way to strategic management and planning courses, the balance between technical and non-technical training is steadily improving.

Training, however, has limitations. Its practical value to an organisation is contingent on a variety of factors. The impact depends not only on the relevancy and quality of the training supplied, but also on the ability of the trainee to translate what may be fairly theoretical information in a classroom context into practical lessons for the organisation. The primary limitation is that by developing individual skills rather than tackling organisational problems, its impact can be superficial. It is often difficult for an individual to return to an 'untrained' organisation, and apply what has been learned (James 1994a). This resistance to change can be partially overcome by training several individuals from the same agency, so that the cumulative impact of learning may have a greater influence throughout the organisation.

In many African countries, the shortage of appropriate, locally tailored courses for the NGO sector means that foreign training is often the only viable option. Sending staff to training institutes abroad can be costly, and financial limitations restrict the number that can be trained in this way. Restricted access to overseas training can create fierce competition within an agency, and favouritism in selection is not uncommon. In some cases, offers of overseas courses are used as a reward for loyalty or are doled out to the more senior members of the organisation.

The reliance on training as the primary tool for capacity building illustrates a skills development bias in response to organisational weaknesses. While attractive for its immediate and concrete output, a lack of individual skills is rarely a leading causal factor in organisational problems, and the immediate response of providing training can allow more fundamental problems to be overlooked. Training can be made more effective by developing a needs-based human resource development plan. To contribute systematically to a coherent process of organisational development, training must respond not only to the individual training needs of staff members, but must relate these to the overall needs of the organisation. It should contribute to organisational learning and knowledge as well as building up individual skill and expertise within the agency.

Funding Specific Technical-Physical Inputs

The performance of Southern NGOs can sometimes be improved by providing physical or technical inputs. If carefully targeted and linked to an organisational assessment, these inputs can address organisational bottlenecks inhibiting effective performance.

But, physical inputs do not necessarily build capacity, and many Northern NGOs mistake the provision of any type of resource as a capacity building exercise. Physical or technical inputs need to be based on an understanding of organisational or service delivery constraints. Providing vehicles to an NGO, for example, acts to increase the frequency of staff visits to clients, contributing to improved information gathering and more efficient service delivery. Similarly, technical weaknesses can be remedied through advisory or technical support. Other inputs may include library resources, computers and software, and physical resources such as basic office equipment.

This type of problem-solving capacity building approach may be used as an important complement to project funding. The impact of providing technical or physical inputs, however, is generally limited to enhancing service delivery functions, rather than building wider organisational capacity and long-term viability.

Volunteers/Secondments

The role of the expatriate 'expert' volunteer is in question. Concern exists that the continuing influx of foreign aid workers has been prioritised at the expense of strengthening the local skills base and developing local organisational capacity. In response to these concerns, the role of volunteers in overseas development is being adapted in order to develop, rather than supplant, local skills. Volunteers are now less often working directly in the field, and are instead working to assist local organisations by imparting essential skills and knowledge to their local counterparts.

Agencies sending volunteers face the challenge of defining the role these external actors should play to ensure maximum benefit for the host NGO. Whereas in the past volunteers primarily transferred technical skills, recently they have begun to address issues relating to NGO management and organisational development. These roles, however, raise their own particular set of problems. The dilemma for temporary, external advisors, whether they are volunteers, seconded staff, or visiting donor NGO staff, is to what extent to adopt a prescriptive and proactive role in solving problems, or whether to remain in a purely facilitative role. At either end of the spectrum, the role of the advisor must be that of a trainer transferring skills, rather than simply performing a task and replacing an employee. In order to perform their facilitative role, volunteers must be able to remain semi-detached from the internal organisational culture and conflicts. Close day-to-day involvement within an organisation can make this exceedingly difficult.

With the development of appropriate and clear parameters, volunteers can act not only to transfer skills but to facilitate wider organisational change.

Management Advice and Consultants

As awareness within the NGO sector grows about the value of good management practices, Northern NGOs are increasingly offering on-going management advice to their implementing partners. In most cases, this input on management issues consists of informal advice and suggestions offered within the context of a friendly relationship. This informal contribution can be useful, but in order to tackle more serious difficulties, most NGOS could benefit from more substantive and structured input on management issues. In these cases, it is often preferable to use experienced management consultants with the knowledge and expertise to guide and advise NGOs on improving organisational structures, systems, and policies.

Management consultancy services can be used effectively to address particular organisational needs. This differs from organisational development consultancy in that it is prescriptive in proposing changes and is designed to tackle specific management areas. An organisation faced with problems resulting from inefficient channels of information, for example, can benefit from assistance in designing an information and feedback system. This type of task-specific management consultancy can be an invaluable source of objective and skilled advice for an NGO.

Organisational Development Consultancies

Organisational development consultancies have only recently been recognised within the NGO sector as a potentially effective means of strengthening organisational capacity. They address organisational and operational capacities in an integral fashion, and seek to facilitate a process of self-assessment and instigate a process of organisational change and improvement.

Organisational development differs from traditional management consultancy discussed above in that it is not designed to tackle a specific problem, or address a particular aspect of the organisation. Instead, it helps the organisation focus and recognise its own mission and identity, understand its own organisational and managerial constraints, and consider ways in which these can be eased. Ideally, a consultant in this field will equip the organisation with the skills needed to recognise and solve its own problems. (The application of organisational development consultancy to enterprise development agencies will be discussed in greater depth in Chapter Seven).

Information Flows and Resources

Access to information is an important resource for NGOs. Small enterprise development agencies need to be aware of advances in operational aspects of credit or training delivery, as well as remaining in touch with wider debates in the field. Access to information is particularly limited for Southern NGOs which generally have little contact with NGOs working in similar areas outside their geographical region. Northern NGOs can strengthen their partners by disseminating information about innovative programmes and successful techniques, and providing resources that enhance understanding of wider development issues and the roles of NGOs. It should be recognised that Northern NGOs have access to a vast reservoir of information and data, publications and training materials, which can only be accessed by Southern NGOs with great difficulty.

Examples of how Northern NGOs can encourage the dissemination of information include paying for subscriptions to relevant journals, providing funding for library resources, funding visits to conferences and other events, and supporting NGO networks which could provide an institutional home for databases and libraries. In addition, it is important to build the research capacity of Southern NGOs and encourage them to publish. Beneficial information flows need not be one directional, but should also ensure that knowledge and information gathered in the developing countries is made available to Northern NGOs.

Accompaniment Services

A more innovative approach to offering on going advisory services to Southern NGOs is 'accompaniment', in which a consultant is hired to provide intermittent advice to a project or Southern NGO over a period of time (James 1994a). Technical, project-based accompaniment is currently the norm, but it is an innovative method which also has the potential to be an effective tool for organisational development. A skilled and experienced management consultant could cost-effectively offer advice over a period of one to two years, providing objective guidance about the overall direction of the agency and its programmes, and on management and administrative matters. This option has the advantage of drawing on local expertise which is independent of the influence of the donor.

Box 6.2 Institutional Development Activities

- Core Funding
  - encourage autonomy from donors, promote self-funding strategies

- Redefining Partnership
  - encourage decision-making power of partners, undertake joint activities and mutual evaluations

- South-South Linkages
  - support exchanges, visits, conferences

- Developing NGO Resource Organisations
  - support NGO resource centres, networks

- Lobbying
  - advocacy for positive NGO legislative frameworks

Source: INTRAC 1994

6.3 INSTITUTIONAL DEVELOPMENT OF THE NGO SECTOR

Although this study focuses on capacity building approaches for individual partner organisations, these programmes are but one component of the broader objective of encouraging the institutional development of the NGO sector as a whole. Institutional development is not concerned with individual NGO performance, but seeks to foster the role of the sector in socio-economic and political development. Northern NGOs and donors are formulating strategies at three levels to support the wider sector. First, are interventions designed to strengthen the autonomy and capacity of a diverse range of NGOs in socio-economic development. At a second level are efforts to encourage greater collaboration and coordination among NGOs at both a national and regional level. A third level of approaches attempt to shape the relationship between state and NGO sector, either by lobbying national governments for favourable legislation or assisting local NGOs to develop their capacity to influence policy. A partial list of institutional development activities that further these objectives is found in Box 6.2.

Level One: Strengthening Southern NGOs
In addition to capacity building interventions and partner financing, the autonomy and strength of the indigenous NGO sector can be initiated by developing more equal partnerships between North and South.

Many Northern agencies are taking practical steps to change the parameters of the traditional donor-recipient relationship. Some larger agencies, for example, are introducing flexible funding agreements with their long-term and most trusted partners. Novib (The Netherlands Organisation for International Development Cooperation), for example, has implemented a programme of institutional funding with some of its Latin American partners. Under this agreement, Novib provides a grant designed to cover both institutional costs and programme activities, on the basis of generally agreed parameters. The recipient NGO is able to use this funding as it wishes, and is accountable to Novib retroactively (James 1994a). The provision of core funding, moreover, provides an NGO with the financial security that it needs to engage in long-term planning.

In a related issue, Northern NGOs can take steps to devolve decision-making power back to Southern partners. Rather than imposing a predetermined set of policies on Southern NGOs, negotiating funding conditions, reporting requirements and timetables allows the partner to have input into the decision making process and feel valued. It should be recognised that Northern NGOs indirectly control a variety of day-to-day activities through strict reporting requirements and timetables set to suit Northern NGOs rather than the implementing partner. Northern NGOs can develop flexible policies adapted to suit the needs of a variety of partner organisations without sacrificing accountability.

A further way to promote a more equal relationship is to establish mechanisms to ensure partner input on key strategic issues facing Northern NGOs.

71

Increasing communication about organisational issues and the identification of priority areas is one way. Incorporating Southern NGO staff on Northern boards or strategic planning sessions can ensure that Northern NGOs remain responsive to their partners on the ground. Mutual evaluations, moreover, can provide Northern NGOs with important feedback from their partners regarding their own performance.

Level Two: South-South Linkages, Networks and Local NGO Support Organisations

NGOs need to promote South-South information flows. Most "expert" advice and current information channels flow from North to South. It is equally important to promote inter-agency communication among Southern NGOs within or across geographic regions. Enhancing South-South information flows can facilitate the sharing of new methodologies, feasibility studies, sector analyses or other research, enabling NGOs to tap into a rich source of local information from similar organisations. Northern NGOs will encourage ties among Southern NGOs by supporting conferences, Southern based publications, staff exchanges and formal NGO networks.

NGO networks provide a mechanism for inter-agency collaboration and coordination. Networks represent the NGO sector *vis-à-vis* governments and donors, and can provide an institutional home for facilities such as libraries and databases for the use of the sector as a whole. Such networks may also be sector specific. There are cases of small enterprise focused NGO networks, (for example, The Consortium of Organisations in Support of Small and Microenterprises, (COPEME), in Peru), in which the majority of agencies operating in the sector are represented. Experience shows task specific networks to be effective in providing focused and specialised services to members.

In addition to networks, NGO support organisations able to meet the needs of local NGOs are essential to the development of strong and mature sector in developing countries. These include resource centres, such as the *NGO Resource Centre* in Pakistan and *El Taller* in Tunisia that aim to provide appropriate training, advice, policy development and other services to local NGOs. Donors should support these emerging local organisations that seek to provide appropriate services to the NGO sector.

Level Three: Lobbying Activities

Efforts to promote the institutional development of the NGO sector in Africa must also encompass the wider political and economic environment. Many NGOs struggle to exist in unfavourable or openly hostile operating environments. Northern NGOs and donors can attempt to influence governments to

72

promote a positive and less restricted policy environment for NGOs. NGO autonomy in many countries is limited and they must therefore actively lobby for legislative frameworks which ensure a degree of autonomy from government control. In order to defend the needs of the poor effectively, NGOs need to be able to adopt a critical stance and remain free of fear of repression. As part of the 'good governance' agenda, Northern NGOs, governments and multilateral agencies are recognising that promoting an independent and active civil society is essential for social and economic development (Clayton 1994).

The institutional development of the NGO sector, therefore, is not merely about supporting individual partner NGOs. Northern NGOs and donors with a serious interest in strengthening the capacity and effectiveness of Southern NGOs must consider the macro-level environment which strongly conditions and defines the role of NGOs. Favourable policy environments might include, for example:

- permanent structures for dialogue and coordination
- involvement of NGOs in government committees
- simplified registration procedures
- tax relief on charitable donations. (Campbell 1989:8)

Improvements in the legislation and regulations governing the NGO sector can strengthen their position in society enabling them to fulfil their roles more effectively.

6.4 PROVIDERS OF CAPACITY BUILDING SERVICES

One problem raised by the growing involvement of Northern NGOs in capacity building is the shortage of experienced service providers. Most capacity building inputs require a degree of management or technical expertise usually held only by specialist service providers.In Africa, new sources of capacity building services are steadily emerging, offering an alternative to services from the North. These local resources include NGO specialist institutions, such as resource centres and networks, as well as consultancy services, from either individuals or specialist organisations. Their ability to provide services relevant to the realities and challenges facing the NGO sector varies widely. The most important service providers are listed in Box 6.3.

Individual Consultants
Throughout Africa and in other developing regions, there is a growing pool of local consultants with experience in the NGO sector. The existence of highly

---

BOX 6.3 Capacity Building Service Providers

- Individual Consultants
- Commercial Management Consultancy Firms
- NGO Consultancy Organisations
- Local Management Schools
- Southern and Northern Training Centres
- NGO Resource Centres
- NGO Networks

Source: INTRAC 1994

---

motivated and skilled individuals, offering both local knowledge and development expertise, will allow for a more sustainable process of development with reduced external intervention. Many Northern NGOs now engage the services of local consultants in place of more costly expatriates whenever possible.

The vast majority of African consultants, however, are skilled in traditional development sectors, such as community development work or agronomy. There is an extremely limited number of consultants working with NGOs on management and administrative issues. The shortage of management consultants in the NGO sector highlights the need for Northern NGOs, and especially official donors, to sponsor programmes which upgrade the skills of local consultants seeking to become involved in organisational development or management consultancy specifically for NGOs. The success of many capacity building programmes is determined by the knowledge and facilitation skill of the consultant involved. Increasing the availability and quality of consultants available to NGOs can contribute to the institutional development of the sector.

Finding appropriate local consultants is often difficult, particularly for those agencies without field offices who cannot readily access local resources. Where appropriate local consultants do not exist, or for those agencies based entirely in the North, expatriate management consultants may be the only viable option. While it is true that the pool of organisational development consultants for the voluntary sector in the North is also limited, there has been a gradual but steady increase in the number of people skilled in NGO management issues. In the short term, NGOs wishing to contract organisational development consultancy in the South may have to continue to rely on expatriates.

Commercial Management Consultancy Firms

An alternative to individual management consultants are commercial management consultancy firms, which are found in many developing countries (Fowler *et al.* 1992). Organisations such as Price Waterhouse and Coopers and Lybrand are responding to the growing demand for services to the non-profit sector. Their high fees are normally only within reach of official and bilateral agencies, and they have been used, with mixed results, for organisational restructuring and financial audits. The valuable expertise of commercial firms in the areas of finance and accounting has been drawn on with considerable success. Their effectiveness beyond this limited role, however, is questionable. Many consultants, drawn from an exclusively commercial background, generally lack an understanding of the value base of the NGO sector. In addition, tendency of the larger firms to assign their younger and more inexperienced staff to NGO contracts, leading some to conclude that their fees often outweigh performance (James 1994b).

NGO Focused Management Consultancy Organisations

A few smaller, NGO-focused consultancy firms have emerged in some African countries. Matrix in Kenya and Symacon in Zimbabwe are examples of this growing trend. These consultancy organisations have either a full or partial focus on NGOs, and are staffed by consultants with previous experience in the sector. They are more likely to have a deeper understanding of development issues and share the same value base. As with any consultancy, the quality of the intervention is largely dependent upon the skill and commitment of the individual consultant assigned to the contract. As the market for NGO-focused services continues to expand, the supply of these services is likely to grow to meet this demand. At present, however, there are only a handful of specialist NGO management consultancy organisations on the African continent.

Local Management Schools

In contrast to the relative shortage of management consultants, many African countries have respected and well established management schools. While most of them have a public administration and commercial focus, some schools are forging links with the NGO sector. Those that offer training and consultancy services to the NGO sector, for example, include the Kenya Institute of Management, the Ghana Institute of Management and Public Administration, the Management Training and Advisory Centre in Uganda. Their strengths lie in training in the more technical aspects of management and administration, such as accounting, although they can also offer training in strategic planning and other management areas.

As with commercial management consultants, the lack of an NGO focus may diminish the effectiveness of the services provided. Despite this drawback, management schools remain an underutilised local resource for NGOs that offers a cost-effective alternative to overseas training.

Northern and Southern Training Centres

Northern NGOs often bring their partners' staff for training in Europe or in the U.S. where NGO focused courses in both management and technical issues are widely available. There is a wider range of courses being offered, and courses appropriate to the specific needs of an NGO are more likely to be found overseas. Overseas training has some advantages. It exposes Southern NGO staff to new ideas and information. It also provides an opportunity for staff to meet their counterparts in similar organisations in other parts of the world. The importance of benefits derived from networking should not be undervalued. It also offers course participants the necessary space and time away from their own NGO to reflect on and assess their work.

Local NGO training centres are now emerging in Africa and elsewhere. The combined advantages of lower costs and context-specific training make local training centres an attractive capacity building service provider where they exist. Examples include Voluntary Agencies Development Assistance in Kenya and Organisational Training and Development Ltd in Zimbabwe (WUS 1994).

NGO Resource Centres

NGO resource centres are non-profit organisations established to provide services to the NGO sector. This is a relatively new concept, and there are very limited number of centres in existence, particularly in the South. These organisations work both at the organisational level, providing services to individual NGOs, and at a strategic level, addressing issues of interest to all NGOs. Their advantage lies in being located within the sector, enabling them to remain responsive to the relevant needs facing the sector and develop appropriate support services. Resource centres can also play an essential research and information dissemination role by developing the capacity to engage in research on issues of strategic importance to the sector (Fowler 1992).

NGO Networks

NGO networks are proliferating throughout Africa, Asia and Latin America. They provide a forum in which NGOs can identify common interests and engage in collaborative activities. Their strength lies in activities at the strategic level, primarily acting as representative bodies of the NGO sector in negotiating with governments, donors and other entities. NGO networks also sponsor conferences and training courses designed to strengthen member agencies.

They can play an important role in the institutional development of the sector, by raising awareness within the NGO community regarding key strategic issues and increasing the negotiating power of the sector.

6.5 SERVICE DELIVERY OPTIONS

Northern NGOs have traditionally engaged directly in the capacity building of their local partners by offering informal advice and support in addition to project funding. This type of partner-to-partner support is conducted primarily through extended staff field visits, and advice on technical and organisational issues. Current capacity building approaches differ from past efforts in that they are based more on explicit external interventions that draw on professional service providers. There are two ways in which services can be procured. First, and most commonly, the donor NGO contracts the supplier directly to provide services to the local NGO. This approach has clear advantages and is preferred by most Northern NGOs for its efficiency and cost-effectiveness. Most importantly, it allows the NGO funding the capacity building service a greater degree of accountability by making the service provider directly responsible to the funder. This degree of accountability and control is important to many NGOs when considering diverting funds from projects to more intangible services.

These advantages are primarily to the benefit of the donor. Hiring suppliers directly can have an adverse impact on the development of the capacity building sector in the long term by making suppliers sensitive to the needs and demands of donors rather than of the NGOs which they are trying to serve (Fowler *et al.* 1992). In addition, donors can use the service provider to fulfil their agenda and address the needs perceived by the donor rather than the local agency. Although this control is largely exerted for reasons related to accountability, in practice this constrains the autonomy of Southern partners. The second, and preferable option, is for Northern NGOs to simply provide funding, while allowing their partners to to select and hire their own capacity building services. Northern NGOs should become more responsive to the needs of their partners and help them access the capacity building services they desire.

6.6 CONCLUSIONS

Northern NGOs have in the past relied largely on their staff to offer informal support and advice to their implementing partner organisations. Most NGOs, both in the North and in the South, require more systematic organisational capacity building interventions to tackle their problems and become stronger as organisations. In response to the growing demand for skilled, specialist services, an increasing range of providers of capacity building services is gradually emerging in both the North and South. Northern NGOs should become aware of the availability of services in the countries in which they work, and seek skilled, specialist inputs rather than relying solely on informal advice by their own staff.

This chapter briefly reviewed the most common capacity building inputs and discussed the primary capacity building providers found in most developing countries. The following lessons can be drawn from the previous discussion:

First, no single capacity building input is sufficient to guarantee improved organisational or technical performance. In order to make significant changes in the capacities and viability of an organisation, an on-going organisational development approach that carefully combines a series of inputs is required. This assumes a long-term commitment to the process on behalf of both the donor NGO and recipient partner organisation. As interventions become more ambitious in their organisational objectives, the degree of difficulty, frequency of contact, and length of the interventions increases greatly.

Second, official donors and Northern NGOs need to prioritise institutional development strategies that increase the availability and quality of capacity building services in the South. A supportive environment for NGOs does not only mean positive and beneficial legal and political frameworks, but also a network of support institutions that facilitate their role in development. A combination of development strategies operating at different levels are necessary for the development of strong and viable local NGO sectors. Policies for the institutional development of the sector are a necessary, complementary activity to the capacity building of individual organisations. In addition to networks that encourage collaboration among NGOs, assistance to NGO resource organisations and training centres can create a support system that provides NGOs with permanent access to training, information and consultancy services.

Third, although there are few specialist capacity building service providers in developing countries, there are other types of organisations with skills and knowledge from which the NGO sector can draw. Local resources, such as commercial consultancy firms or management schools have not been adequately utilised by the NGO sector. Although these organisations are not specifically targeted at the NGO community, they have valuable skills to offer.

These commercially-oriented organisations may be particularly useful for the small enterprise development sector, which requires a high level of financial management capacity. However, these service providers vary in the quality of assistance and their ability to design and implement a support programme. Northern NGOs must act cautiously and prudently when selecting them. Additionally, these processes must be subject to careful assessment, monitoring and evaluation in order to determine their impact on organisational performance.

Fourth, Northern NGOs and donors should provide funding that enables Southern NGOs to engage the services of capacity building service providers. Allowing Southern NGOs to select and manage the process will ensure that suppliers remain responsive to the needs of NGOs rather than donors.

Part Four

Capacity Building Case Studies

7

Organisational Development Support for NGOs

7.1 INTRODUCTION

In the complex and turbulent African environment, NGOs must adapt to rapidly changing political and economic circumstances, and respond appropriately to the evolving needs of the communities with which they work. The stronger NGOs are as organisations, the better equipped they are to anticipate changes in the environment and ensure a close match between their programmes and the needs of their target groups. In order to manage these external factors, NGOs need first to be competent internally, with a clear sense of purpose and well functioning management systems.

Organisational development interventions lay the foundation for effective programme implementation by increasing an NGO's overall organisational capacity. In contrast, most capacity building inputs, such as training, target specifically defined capacities and are designed to improve a problem area. However effective such an intervention may be, an approach which addresses particular problems in isolation will fail to engage with important underlying issues relating to an organisation's culture, values, mission and leadership style.It is sometimes necessary to reject a piecemeal approach to capacity building and consider the totality of an organisation if genuine overall improvements are to be made.

Organisational development support is most often provided in the form of long-term and intermittent consultancy. Management consultants are not only useful as external experts hired to provide solutions to immediate problems or crises. External facilitation can help an NGO to identify its own priorities and to introduce appropriate and necessary changes in organisational structure and behaviour.

This chapter discusses some of the key principles of organisational development, and considers two contrasting cases of capacity building interventions which include an organisational development consultancy.

7.2 ORGANISATIONAL DEVELOPMENT: THEORY AND PRACTICE

Organisational development consultancy differs from prescriptive and problem-solving management consultancy. Task focused consultancies, designed to obtain a specific output from the consultants, can be effective in tackling particular organisational or operational issues, but are unlikely to initiate organisation-wide changes. Organisational development consultants, in contrast, do not address specific procedural or system-related problems, but provide external facilitation to help an NGO to identify and improve its organisational weaknesses. NGOs must participate in the development of solutions to their problems, and the role of the consultant should be to help the NGO to develop the skills that would enable it to recognise and address future problems. If correctly and sensitively conducted, change is neither imposed or prescribed. Instead the NGO is encouraged to develop systems suited to its unique needs and requirements.

Organisational development interventions are also more comprehensive. Their focus is not restricted to changes in one particular department or system area, but encompasses the wider issues of organisational identity, culture and behaviour. This wider perspective makes it a useful tool for initiating far-reaching and long lasting improvements in organisational and operational capacity. These rather ambitious aims invariably entail a lengthy and complex intervention, whose success is contingent on a variety of factors.

First and foremost of these is the commitment and motivation of the recipient NGO. A reluctant organisation is unlikely to make a genuine effort to identify and acknowledge its own weaknesses, or have the resolve to undergo an often difficult process of change. It is also important for the entire organisation to be committed, from the highest echelon of management to the most distant field worker. Neither the consultant nor the donor can impose change on an unwilling NGO. Organisational development interventions will succeed only if the organisation is committed and capable of taking it forward on its own initiative.

A second key variable is the skill and insight of the consultant. An external facilitator must be able to elicit a variety of views, and be able to interpret events. He or she must be aware of the interests of the relevant stakeholders and reconcile them when possible. Hidden agendas do often exist and latent conflict may emerge. While in theory the role of the consultant is primarily facilitative in leading the NGO through a process of making decisions about organisational change and improvement, the consultant is often placed in the position of having to reject a completely neutral role and influence decisions.

Unfortunately, skilled organisational development consultants with experience in the NGO sector are not widely available. In some countries, such as the South African and Zimbabwean cases presented here, there are experienced, specialist NGO management consultancy organisations. In most countries, however, this is still the exception. In cases where experienced consultants are lacking, alternatives include bringing in local commercial consultants, or identifying expatriate consultants from neighbouring countries.

The commitment required for organisational development eclipses that of other capacity building interventions with more limited objectives. Genuine improvements in organisational culture and behaviour call for lengthy and frequent advisory inputs. For these reasons, medium-term and intermittent consultancy support is usually required, lasting anywhere from a few months to one or two years.

Organisational development interventions begin by understanding the inner most characteristics of an organisation, such as identity, values, purpose, and gradually work towards operational issues. (See Figure 3.1 which illustrates the directionality of organisational development relative to that of technical capacity building processes.) Although the theory and practice of organisational development originated within the commercial sector, it may in fact of particular value to the non-profit sector, where issues of values and identity are essential. Strategic planning, which enables purpose to be related to the environment and translated into action, follows coherently only if the identity is clear.

This section has discussed some of the principles of organisational development in theory. As ever, translating pure theoretical models into practice is difficult. In reality, organisational development is an umbrella word for a variety of interventions, of which a deeply-engaged consultancy is but one approach. A pure organisational development consultancy – one that remains facilitative, addresses core identity issues, and is ongoing – is still fairly uncommon in the NGO sector.

This chapter examines organisational development in practice by comparing two case studies in which the consultants were assigned very different roles. The cases of the Budiriro Development Association in Zimbabwe and the Triple Trust Organisation in South Africa differed both in the motivations for instigating a consultancy and in the way the process was managed and controlled. These cases illustrate the basic principles of managing organisational development interventions, and also highlight some potential pitfalls.

7.3 THE TRIPLE TRUST ORGANISATION, SOUTH AFRICA

The Triple Trust Organisation (TTO) of South Africa has undergone tremen-

dous growth since its inception in 1988. The initial success of its training programme for the unemployed in the Cape Town area rapidly attracted the attention of both international donors and local corporate sponsors. Although the
increased amount of funding in this early period enabled TTO to expand the
range of services offered to clients, it also generated some organisational
problems associated with rapid growth. The main challenges facing TTO,
rather surprisingly, were not the central questions of strategy or a loss of focus
often experienced by young and rapidly expanding organisations. Instead,
problems relating to overall organisational structure and deteriorating staff-
management relations gradually became apparent. In 1993, these factors
prompted senior management to decide to slow the rate of growth, consolidate
the organisation and address these internal issues. After a lengthy process of
consultation with staff, TTO enlisted the services of local consultants to help
it reassess and improve its organisational structure and behaviour. TTO provides an interesting – but fairly atypical – case of an organisational development process initiated and controlled entirely by the recipient NGO.

The Triple Trust Organisation: History and Objectives
The Triple Trust Organisation was set up in 1988 in response to the massive
problem of unemployment in South Africa. Founded on the premise that people have the right to a dignified manner of earning a living, and recognising
the importance of encouraging self-sufficiency and personal motivation, TTO
assists those who wish to escape from unemployment and poverty by establishing a micro- or small enterprise.

The limited income-earning opportunities of many unemployed people is
due in part to their lack of appropriate and marketable skills. Despite the
importance of formal education and technical skills, however, it is clear that
technical training alone leaves trainees insufficiently equipped to make a successful transition from unemployment to sustainable self-employment. TTO's
founders therefore endeavoured to design a pragmatic model of support to
meet the extensive and varied needs of aspiring entrepreneurs. Although technical training is a central component, the programme also aims to develop the
wide variety of personal skills and knowledge needed to set up a successful
micro-enterprise. The assistance programme is currently comprised of training, credit, marketing assistance, and advisory support.

The first phase of the programme focuses on skills acquisition to help
aspiring entrepreneurs to develop marketable technical skills, and also to gain
personal confidence and a spirit of self-reliance. The training courses aim to
develop multi-purpose technical skills that enable trainees to manufacture a
variety of products, rather than focusing on a specific skill which might tie
them to a single item. Currently, eight-week training courses are offered in

sewing, leather work, knitting and butchery. Trainees must also enrol in a business skills course which features an innovative business simulation game, known as BEST (Business Expenses Savings Training). BEST enhances learning by allowing trainees to practice essential business concepts, such as resource allocation (i.e., choices between personal income, savings, or reinvestment in the business), pricing, costing and marketing.

As graduates move on from the training courses to establish their own economic activity, they are entitled to apply for a micro-loan to cover their start-up costs of capital equipment and initial working capital. Advisory support is also offered during the difficult, initial period of creating and consolidating their enterprise. The marketing division, for example, is continuously involved in identifying new markets and product opportunities, and in some cases acts as liaison between producers and formal sector markets. This early assistance in marketing, it is hoped, provides a market base from which the entrepreneur is expected to follow through on his/her own. All graduate trainees are also entitled to receive mentoring support and business counselling from volunteers and staff to help them address any problems their business may be facing. The mentoring programme not only provides essential on-site business advice, but also helps to break the isolation which individual entrepreneurs may feel. After approximately six months, the entrepreneur is progressively weaned from the programme in order to reduce and ultimately eliminate any dependency on these services.

Rapid Growth and Organisational Stress
This comprehensive package of services has proved effective in assisting a significant number of unemployed people to create employment for themselves and for others. As with most NGOs, TTO's immediate focus was on output; specifically, on improving programme content and assisting as many people as possible. TTO successfully attracted new sources of funding, established new departments, and opened more training centres. In the period between 1988 and 1994, TTO rapidly evolved from a small organisation with 4 full-time staff members, to a large, decentralised organisation with a staff of 70, operating 20 training centres throughout the Cape Town area (see Table 7.1).

Rapid growth immediately began to generate stresses within the organisation. Rapid expansion has considerable organisational implications. Growth invariably requires changes in management style and the institutionalisation of policies and procedures. Informal decision-making is advantageous to small agencies by allowing for flexibility and responsiveness, but can be inappropriate for larger organisations. In order to ensure accountability in agencies with multiple branches, like TTO, formal financial and management systems are essential. Without long-term institutional planning to address these necessary organisational changes, decisions and policies are in danger of being made by default rather than by design. In TTO's case, the opening of 19 new training centres in a six year period left little time to devote to long-term strategic and institutional planning. Many important decisions regarding the use of resources, internal restructuring and staff development were being made in an *ad hoc* fashion, as planning was unable to keep up with the rate of growth. By 1993, the limitations of the growth-first approach had become apparent, and TTO executives initiated an organisational self-assessment process.

Table 7.1 Triple Trust: Indicators of Growth		
	1988	**1994**
Staff	4	70
Training Centres	1	20
Budget	R 100,000	R 3.5 million
Trainees	200	1300

The Self-Assessment Process

TTO began a period of organisational self-assessment in 1993. Issues of concern were brainstormed and then categorised into four groups. Four task groups were established in the areas of communication, terms of employment, structural change and cultural diversity. They met regularly to discuss some of the perceived weaknesses of the organisation within the four broad themes and to debate how these could be constructively addressed.

All staff were required to participate in a group, and they were encouraged to select the topic about which they felt most passionate. As the groups progressed in their discussions, a core group emerged from each task group and acted to finalise and summarise the conclusions reached. Although the larger task groups were established for a limited time, to date, a number of sub-committee groups looking at specific issues within the four broad categories continue to function.

An organisational assessment process can be full of tension, and the case of the Triple Trust was no exception. Identifying organisational problems requires accessing people's different perceptions from all areas of the organisation and encouraging them to express their reservations or disagreements over policy, structure and direction. Actively unearthing latent conflict is inherently a stressful process, but is the first step in developing a plan to resolve these problems.

Despite the inevitable conflict which emerged, the mere process of discussing problem areas had a positive effect on staff morale. First, it created a structured forum for staff to express their views on a variety of issues; and second, the fact that the task groups had been established led staff to recognise that management was concerned and interested in their opinions.

Organisational Constraints

During discussions and negotiations throughout the year-long process, a variety of interrelated issues emerged which were of concern to both staff and management. Although some of the problems identified were specific and operational in nature, many dealt with important issues at a broader strategic level. Amongst the most important issues raised were the following:

(1) TTO felt the need to confront and recognise the devastating impact apartheid has had on individuals, both black and white, within the organisation. It was important to come to terms with the context of racism and acknowledge how these difficult conditions may have shaped and affected the organisation as a whole. Central to this process was a two-day workshop led by an outside facilitator, on 'Unlearning Racism'. The act of directly confronting and debating these issues not only helped individuals to grow and mature on a personal level, but it is hoped that it also had a positive impact on organisational culture and behaviour.

(2) Among the most consequential issues to emerge from the task groups was a confirmation of earlier indications that the organisational structure had grown rigid and hierarchical in order to cope with the logistical requirements of operating 20 training centres. While services were successfully decentralised, with training centres located in township community centres throughout the Cape Town area, most decision-making and policy-making functions remained centralised in headquarters. As a result of the spontaneous way in which expansion happened, there had been a gradual and almost imperceptible evolution towards a more vertical organisational structure. The task force highlighted a need to revise and adapt the way systems, policies and procedures were made.

The problem of excessive centralisation is clearly linked to the issue of participation. Communication between headquarters and the training centres worsened as the number of field offices grew, in essence enlarging the apparent gap between staff and management. There were indications that this contributed to a deterioration in morale. During in-depth discussions it emerged that staff felt distant from decision-making and planning processes. Field staff felt as if they were not a valued part of the organisation.

There is, arguably, a natural tendency for organisations to become more centralised as they grow, and for some NGOs, this is the acceptable price of expansion. TTO, however, believes strongly in the value of staff participation and seeks to maintain a flat organisational structure with substantial input from field staff into the planning process. This issue became the focal point of the organisational development consultancy which followed.

(3) Greater commitment to staff training and the development of effective human resource development plans were also priorities. Investing in staff training is sometimes perceived by NGOs to be an unnecessary expense that diverts funds from the target communities. In an effort to keep non-project costs down, NGOs are sometimes wary of investing in staff development programmes. However, as TTO realised, this is a short sighted view, as the skills and capacities of staff determine the quality of the programme. Upgrading the skills and knowledge of staff not only boosts the overall morale of the organisation but also results in improved services.

(4) Staff and management also expressed concern over possible unintended consequences of rapid expansion on programme effectiveness. There is often a tension between scale and quality, and while TTO aimed to assist as many people as possible, it sought to achieve an appropriate balance between quantity and quality.

Some trade-offs are inevitable as a programme extends its coverage and seeks to remain cost effective. TTO, for example, found that it had to make significant changes in its mentoring programme as the number of trainees swelled from 200 to 1,300. Initially, the mentoring programme had a sufficient staff-student ratio to advise all graduates on a one-to-one basis. As the programme grew and staff were unable to advise all graduates on a personal level, volunteers were trained to provide small business advice. While these changes in the process and mode of mentoring do not necessarily indicate a poorer calibre of service, TTO worried that decisions had been made in response to the immediate challenges of expansion, rather than as part of a considered and strategic change in the programme. The self-assessment process provided an opportunity to take a step back and consider these issues in a more relaxed and less urgent way. It enabled the organisation as a whole to carefully assess whether trade-offs had been made and if so, whether they were of an acceptable degree.

The concern over possible unintended trade-offs between scale and quality reflected a deeper problem: an insufficient focus on strategy. Staff were too busy 'doing' and reacting to immediate problems, to think, question, plan and analyse. Too tied to the day-to-day requirements of establishing new training centres and launching new training programmes, the organisation was failing to engage with long-term planning issues. The overriding pressures of expansion had consumed the attention and time of staff and management.

(5) Monitoring and evaluation had been receiving insufficient attention. TTO needed to improve its monitoring systems and refine its evaluation processes. Confronted with the challenge of promoting self employment, TTO needed to define its aims and articulate the intended impact on trainees. Providing training, in itself, is not TTO's ultimate objective, and clear criteria by which to measure success were lacking.

(6) Financial stability was also a concern of the agency. Increasing self-reliance and moving towards greater financial independence by generating income was a long-standing aim of the TTO. In addition, it sought to diversify its funding base to minimise the risk of dependency on a few donors.

(7) Open and honest discussions also revealed a need for improved interpersonal relations and team building, to regain the full confidence and loyalty of the staff. The process of engaging openly with each other in the task groups acted as a boost to staff morale. More importantly, it introduced a new culture of better communication and honesty within the organisation.

The Way Forward

The Triple Trust Organisation emerged from the process of self-evaluation with a better understanding of the areas needing improvement, not only in relation to programme performance, but also to its own internal functioning. In addition, the foundation of respect and trust that had been developed equipped TTO to meet the challenges facing the organisation. According to James Thomas, Managing Director, the organisational development priorities pertain to four broad areas:

- *Operational Capacity:* TTO seeks to build its operational capacity and to develop a reliable service delivery mechanism which can reach as many people as possible.

- *Stability:* The organisation aims to strengthen its organisational capacity by addressing issues of staff representation and consultation in management. Developing a horizontal management structure in which field staff have greater input is expected to be one of the key outcomes of the organisational development process.

- *Sustainability:* TTO seeks to increase its self-reliance and financial independence.

- *Excellence:* TTO aims to maintain a high standard of professional excellence and to encourage the development and training of staff.

Emerging from a lengthy and occasionally conflictual process of self-evaluation, the organisation was ready to initiate a slow and careful process of change. It was clear that not only procedures and policies needed to be rectified, but changes made in the organisational culture and decision-making processes. In order to facilitate the process, TTO engaged the services of the Community Development Resource Association (CDRA), a reputable South African organisation that provides organisational development consultancy to the NGO sector. CDRA provides external support and facilitation to assist NGOs in clarifying objectives and in introducing organisational and procedural change.

The decision to bring in external consultants was made cautiously, and considerable time and effort was devoted to finding consultants sympathetic to TTO's beliefs, objectives and values. Commercial consultants with limited experience with the NGO sector were eliminated from consideration early on in the process. The final decision was made not only on the basis of the reputation of the firm, but on the cultural compatibility of the individual consultants. The consultants had to be able to communicate openly with all levels of staff, from senior management to field staff, and to relate to both black and white staff. The CDRA was contracted on an initial three month basis, that would enable TTO to decide whether or not to contract them for further stages of organisational development intervention.

Although TTO chose to undergo this process of self-examination without the coercion or active encouragement of a donor, it was successful in asking an existing donor to fund the costs of the intervention. This donor had specifically committed financial resources to assist the organisation in staff development and agreed that some of their funds could be channelled to cover the costs of this organisational development process. The role of the donor was strictly limited to funding the consultancy and allowing for these non-project costs – not to become involved in the organisational development process itself. The CDRA has been contracted directly by, and reports exclusively to, TTO.

The central focus of the CDRA's involvement was to help TTO to achieve its goal of operating with a more participative management style. The consultancy explored and considered structures which would ensure staff consultation on management decisions and enhance the degree of staff participation in all stages of strategic planning.

These structural issues necessarily require questioning and reconsideration of roles and responsibilities. To what extent should strategic planning be the responsibility of managers in headquarters who have the advantages of distance from day-to-day problems, and time to consider long-term implications and plans? What should be the input of those on the technical side who work more closely with the trainees? These are some of the issues that TTO had to grapple with.

Initially, it was unclear what the CDRA methodology would be, but this became apparent as time went on. They adopted a process with four basic steps:

- examination and redefinition of the organisation's mission
- examination and redefinition of their values
- examination and redefinition of the organisation's structure
- examination and rebuilding of perceptions, feelings and relationships.

The initial phase of CDRA's involvement was designed to elicit the views, concerns and priorities of TTO's staff. In November 1994, CDRA consultants spent three days interviewing members of staff, followed by a full day meeting with senior management. As a result of this intensive survey of staff and management perceptions of culture and organisational structure, CDRA prepared and distributed a report to all staff at the end of December 1994, summarising the organisation's strengths and weaknesses as perceived by staff.

Following the report's presentation, TTO decided that a representative group of staff should spend a week debating the issues raised in the report. The workshop concentrated on the issues raised in the report as they relate to mission and values, and discussed the underlying organisational culture. These were recorded and written up as 'organisational norms' to provide an insight into TTO's culture. This statement of implicit norms, many of which were undesirable, provided a basis for discussion of a set of values by which the organisation should operate. The workshop concluded by committing to paper a vision and values statement, an important step made possible by the guided process of the CDRA, which gave staff the opportunity to express their views, opinions and aspirations.

Having tackled the central issues of mission and values, CDRA then focused on problems relating to organisational structure. Intensive consulting on a residential basis began for a one-week period in January 1995, and included the participation of 40 staff members. CDRA employed individual interviews, small group discussions and full group 'therapy' sessions. The first step was to define the principles upon which the restructuring would be based. After lengthy consultation, the following four objectives were agreed:

- information should be more freely available
- decisions should be taken at a range of different levels
- there should be fewer departments with fewer lines to a central person
- leadership should be wider and more focused.

CDRA then worked jointly with TTO to develop a structure that fulfilled these conditions.

In early 1995, TTO adopted a new organisational structure with five divisions (client contact, client services, administration, public relations, and research and development), each comprised of various departments. The divisions meet regularly to deal with relevant issues at that level. Wider strategic issues are referred to a Leadership Team, comprised of rotating divisional representatives, in addition to the General Manager, Managing Director and Financial Director. To ensure greater participation in decision-making, in practice, the Leadership Team refers as many issues as possible back to the division responsible. The representative nature of the Leadership Team helps bridge the gap between staff and management, and ensures greater participation in strategic and operational decision-making processes.

The organisation has chosen to monitor and assess its own progress through a Process Monitoring Group rather than rely on external consultants. The group meets monthly to monitor and be updated on:

- the general feelings in the organisation in terms of attitudes, culture, identity, values, etc.
- the progress of the subcommittees looking at operational or strategic issues
- the effectiveness of the new structure.

A week of intensive consulting was scheduled with CDRA for June 1995 for the purpose of additional assessment and a possible conclusion to the consulting process.

Outcomes

In the area of sustainability, TTO has made progress in diversifying its funding base since its inception in 1988. The organisation originally acquired a considerable proportion of its funding from the local corporate sector, and later sought to supplement this source of finance with international aid. To contribute to the goal of financial self-sufficiency, a consulting branch has been set up to respond to requests from other NGOs and formal businesses. The consulting department is entirely self-financing, and any profits made are donated back to TTO. Important gains have also been made, for example, by packaging the TTO developed BEST game for sale to other organisations.

Staff training programmes have been implemented, and the technical and management skills of trainers are being upgraded. In the area of operational capacity, continuous efforts are made to evaluate and improve the content of the support offered to emerging entrepreneurs. A Research and Evaluation Department has now been established to ensure reliable and accurate reporting and evaluation of the project. New services, such as the development of independent producers workshop facilities, are being introduced. In areas more directly addressed by the CDRA consultancy, improvements can be seen in three basic areas:

First, mission and value statements have been thoroughly discussed, widely debated and committed to paper. A clear identity and mission are important prerequisites for effective strategic planning. Second, the organisational assessment and development process has enabled latent conflict to be acknowledged and resolved where possible. Opportunity for staff to air their opinions, concerns, and priorities has contributed to an atmosphere of trust and loyalty. Third, organisational restructuring has led to a more participatory and flat organisational decision-making structure. It is as yet too early to assess its long-term impact on the organisation and its performance.

The question of how to evaluate these intangible and qualitative factors, as with any organisational development process, is difficult. Specific indicators have not been developed, but the central tasks are clear. The outcome will have been considered a success if decision-making processes are implemented which allow for decisions to be made by consensus. Ultimately though, the indicators of success will be contented staff and improved performance.

The Triple Trust Organisation: Some Lessons Learned
The organisational problems highlighted here are not uncommon to NGOs. It is often the situation that changing circumstances – in this case the growth of funding – can overtake the ability to plan and adapt successfully. What is, perhaps, more uncommon is the degree of self-awareness required to recognise that a period of consolidation is necessary, and the commitment to confront problem areas directly. TTO was sufficiently mature to develop its own plan of organisational strengthening, in which the consultants were one element.

94

This case provides a few important insights as to how an NGO can success-fully manage an organisational development process.

First, investing time and effort into an in-depth assessment process provides a sound basis for organisational development. This case illustrates the value of participatory organisational assessment techniques. An in-depth self-assessment process enabled organisational problems to be accurately pin-pointed and perceptions and concerns to unearthed. With this knowledge, the CDRA was able to guide TTO through its restructuring phase.

Second, a period of introspection can be helpful, as long as the ultimate goal of improving services is not lost. Organisational weaknesses are not always readily apparent. Non-profit organisations are usually reluctant to invest the staff time required to analyse and reflect on the effectiveness of their own management structures. The task force groups entailed an expenditure of staff time, but provided the necessary space and time to take a step back from day-to-day events and consider internal performance. It is important, however, to avoid endless debate about inconsequential or interpersonal issues, and to keep in sight the long-term purpose of the self-assessment exercise, which is an improved capacity to deliver effective and appropriate services to the tar-get group.

Third, growth is not everything. Growth is often a central concern of young or small NGOs, but many are unprepared to manage its impact. Rapid expan-sion invariably places stress on an agency, and usually requires a thorough reconsideration of existing organisational patterns and structures. As alluring as increasing funding may be, many NGOs could benefit from a periodic con-solidation and reflection that allows them to revisit their original aims and objectives.

Fourth, NGOs must be willing to recognise their own internal weaknesses and be able to develop strategies to work through them. This point may appear obvious, but nonetheless needs to be stated. There is a natural reluc-tance on behalf of both individuals and organisations to recognise or accept their own flaws. This case study illustrates that concerted effort is often required to identify clearly the source of problems. The task groups estab-lished by TTO provided a forum for all staff to express their views and express disagreements. This process can be conflictual and difficult, and if handled ineptly can act to deepen the sense of crisis. Identifying problems is only the first step; the greater challenge is to develop a constructive plan to solve them. External facilitation can be useful in this capacity by helping NGOs explore options for improvement.

Fifth, conflict is often latent. Accessing different perceptions within an organisation is an essential part of a self-assessment process, and may reveal underlying friction or dissension which was not otherwise apparent. Staff may have serious concerns which they do not feel comfortable expressing unless an appropriate forum is provided. It is also important that such conflict, when brought into the open, be well facilitated.

Sixth, the role of the consultants should be one element of a wider plan of organisational development. There is a danger that organisational development consultants are brought in, not to facilitate a process, but to direct it. In this case, the role of the external input was only one part a of coordinated, long-term plan of self-assessment, human resource development and restructuring which was already in progress. The consultants were one element of the process, not the central element.

Seventh, NGOs must give importance to finding organisational structures and functions which are appropriate and acceptable to them. TTO values highly an organisational and decision-making structure that is satisfying to all staff, and was willing to invest considerable time and effort to develop such a structure. Not all organisations aim for maximum staff participation in decision-making processes, but it is important for agencies to find modes of working which suit them and their staff.

7.4 SYMACON, ZIMBABWE – SYSTEMS MANAGEMENT CONSULTANCY FOR NGOs

The Budiriro Development Agency (BDA)[2] in Zimbabwe is a membership organisation that provides a range of small enterprise development services to its entrepreneur members. Concern with the BDA's weak performance overall led one of its donors to consider an organisational development intervention to strengthen its organisational capacities. Systems Management Consultancy (Symacon), a private Zimbabwean management consultancy organisation, was contracted by the donor to offer support services and management advice to

[1] This case study is based on a paper presented by Simon Matsvai of Symacon to the workshop, 'Building the Organisational Capacity of Small Enterprise Development Agencies in Africa: Options for Northern NGOs', INTRAC, November 22, 1994, London.

[2] To protect the confidentiality of those involved, the name of the local NGO has been changed.

the BDA. Symacon works principally with NGOs and community-based organisations, but also has worked with government departments, bi- and multilateral agencies, private commercial companies and financial institutions.

BDA History and Objectives

The Budiriro Development Agency (BDA) is a membership organisation founded in 1983 by a group of 15 small businessmen. These entrepreneurs, most of whom were involved in agricultural production, petty trading and metalworking, formed the association in response to their perceived need to access support services for their enterprises. As with many associations, BDA had wide ranging and ambitious aims when initially established. It aimed to assist members in acquiring inputs and raw materials, to provide financial support, and to offer training in production and management skills. The association was also to play a representative role to government on matters concerning access to land and finance.

In addition to providing support services to members' enterprises, the BDA engaged in productive activities to generate income for itself. Its programme contained five components: training, fundraising, financing, tillage services and transport services. The many elements of the programme proved too much for the organisation's administrative, managerial and logistical capacity. More significantly, it reflected a lack of focus and an unclear identity. Concerned by consistently poor performance in many areas, the intervention was initiated a donor, who felt that the BDA could benefit from management and organisational input. Symacon was contracted to conduct an in-depth evaluation and assessment of BDA's organisational and operational capacities, and to facilitate a process of organisational change.

The Diagnostic Process

Symacon believes that management and operational capacities are inextricably linked and must be dealt with in an integrated fashion. The dual objectives of the consultancy were to assist the BDA to identify organisational deficiencies, and to assess and improve its programme capacity.

Symacon has considerable experience in providing such services to NGOs. These consultancies begin with organisational analysis based on a thorough review of the following areas:

- vision, mission and objectives
- organisational capacity in terms of structure, human resource development, and financial strategy
- operating capacity, which includes a review of human, physical, financial and management capacity.

Once the initial diagnostic stage has identified the organisation's weaknesses and constraints, Symacon facilitates planning sessions to help the organisation develop solutions. Symacon remains closely involved in the change effort, providing active advice and assistance throughout the management and organisational changes. When the capacity and stage of development of an organisation suggest that a directive influence is needed, Symacon adopts an active and prescriptive role in the development of management solutions and systems.

Symacon began its consultancy with BDA with a brief review and analysis of the agency's policies and structures. This was conducted principally by revising records and holding one-to-one discussions with key staff and managers. These sessions focused on:

- typical day-to-day operating routines
- decision-making processes as they involve the staff and executive committee
- financial administration systems.

This preliminary understanding of BDA's internal operations prepared the consultants to facilitate in-depth assessment sessions with the agency's leaders.

A series of discussions with the Board of Directors delved further into the BDA's strengths and weaknesses. Symacon attempted to discover where Board members felt deficiencies existed. These sessions were often long and tedious. While they were primarily facilitative in nature, the consultants had to teach many business concepts to the Board members before they could be expected to make decisions. These concepts had to be expressed and discussed in simple and clear terms, because ensuring that Board members understood them was essential for their full participation in the organisational development process. If Symacon had presented its findings in a technocratic, prescriptive report, this might have alienated Board members, rather than engage them with the issues.

The second stage of the assessment process entailed a survey of members to assess the level of demand for BDA's services. Symacon felt that the range of services offered was too wide, and that a better understanding of the needs of members would enable programme activities to be realigned and better focused. This needs assessment was also a way to get members to participate in the process and agree to changes to BDA's programme. Given the legislation governing membership agencies, the executive committee had to consult their members before changes could be made in programme or organisational structure. The findings of the survey were then put to a general meeting of the membership, where it was decided what services the agency should provide.

The general meeting provided a forum for members to debate the focus of the agency and to discuss how existing deficiencies could be overcome. Open and honest discussions, however, were complicated by the BDA's ideology, which shied away from the notion that businesses were motivated by profit and that economic success was important. Members, as well as the executive committee, were hesitant to accept that financial sustainability was appropriate or possible for an NGO.

This diagnostic stage was concluded after a period of months. Symacon's success in gaining an understanding of BDA's organisational strengths and weaknesses was due largely to its intensive review and assessment at three different levels: first, the initial independent review conducted by the consultants; second, the in-depth sessions with the executive committee; and third, the survey of members' needs and subsequent general meeting. This tri-level approach enabled Symacon to elicit perceptions at all levels of the agency.

The Nature of the Problem

BDA experienced many of the strategic difficulties faced by small enterprise development agencies, in addition to the common organisational problems that plague many membership associations. Its main organisational constraints can be loosely grouped into three key areas:

First, BDA suffered from unclear mission and identity. The primary confusion was whether it aimed to be a self-sustaining, profit-oriented service provider or a support organisation offering subsidised services. In addition to providing credit and training on a subsidised basis, BDA also engaged in economic activities meant to generate income for the association. The agency attempted to run the tilling and transport services on a profitable basis, but lacked the business skills and ideological clarity to do so. Both members and leaders within the organisation were wary of adopting a profit-oriented approach to service delivery. Members who had helped found the BDA sometimes resisted paying for services received, and failed to understand the financial implications of their actions on the organisation. It was important for the BDA to clarify its role and objectives and educate its membership regarding the need for a profit-oriented approach to service provision.

Second, BDA's services were poorly matched to the needs of its target group and its capacity to deliver. With poor diagnostic skills, programme design will reflect what the agency wants to do rather than what the members genuinely require. BDA was trying to do too much and everything for its members. The agency had limited capacity to train, fundraise or deliver credit to small enterprises, yet it tried to do so, without much success. Its inability to prioritise objectives and focus the programme more narrowly to suit the real needs of members led to consistently poor performance in many programme areas. A central objective of the subsequent organisational development intervention, therefore, was to develop diagnostic and strategic planning skills. BDA needed to define precisely its objectives and develop a viable strategy to achieve them.

Third, it was apparent that the organisational structure of the agency was not suited for its service delivery and income earning activities. The formal organisational structure was largely political in nature and was designed to develop the democratic systems required of a membership association. The constitution was concerned with issues such as the election of leaders and the rights of members, and failed to address the technical and operational structure. While the roles of elected officials may have been understood, for example, the roles and responsibilities of staff engaged in managing BDA on a day-to-day basis had never been articulated. Management systems at the financial, human resources and operations level were also weak or non-existent. This is not unusual for membership organisations. Tension between the political structure and technical structure can divert attention from service delivery and may restrict the exercise of managerial functions.

It was critical that the BDA go back to fundamentals, by elaborating and clarifying its basic organisational structures, and developing formal management systems and procedures.

The Intervention
Agreeing on a focused programme is a critical precondition of a capacity building process. The next stage was to formulate an intervention strategy in consultation with both the donor and the BDA leadership. Symacon noted that in this case, the donor expected a heightened role and influence in the decision-making process because it had initiated and funded the consultancy. The donor was convinced that there was the potential to strengthen the BDA, so that it could perform the dual functions of delivering effective business development services to its members and operating its own business units. The support and confidence of the donor, despite the obvious organisational crisis, bolstered the BDA and encouraged it to take the capacity building process seriously.

The diagnostic stage revealed the depth of the BDA's organisational problems. The capacity building strategy which was then devised dealt not merely with organisational issues, but also considered strategy and programming issues.

In the area of strategy and programmes, the most urgent need was for BDA to establish priorities and focus its programmes. The donor, consultants and agency were involved in planning sessions to help BDA eliminate those services that had limited impact on the members' enterprises or were beyond the scope of BDA's capacities to deliver effectively. These planning sessions were facilitated by Symacon, who attempted to teach the BDA leadership the steps involved in strategic planning, such as needs assessments methods, programme design and financial planning. While these sessions were fruitful and constructive, BDA's programming capacity could have been further enhanced if the staff participation had been greater. The low level of staff involvement throughout the capacity building process later emerged as one of the most serious constraints of the intervention.

There was clear agreement after these planning sessions that members would benefit most by receiving improved services in three key areas: input supply tillage (for both members and non-members); technical advice on production, planning and operations; and training in management. The credit scheme and transport service were eliminated from the programme.It must be recognised that in a process with many interested stakeholders, hidden agendas and different priorities are likely to emerge. In this case, one of the forces at work here was the donor's preference for maintaining the training element in order to justify the project to the donating constituency back home. It is unclear to what extent this may have influenced the final decision to retain the training programme. What is clear, however, is that the donor was not completely neutral in the decision-making process.

The consultants played an advisory and facilitative role in helping BDA revise its programme, and were involved in:

- putting together a business plan to respond to the demand for services
- defining the inputs required to implement the plan
- defining the training and consultancy components
- costing the programme
- discussing the programme and budget plan with the agency leadership.

The full participation and contribution of BDA leaders in clarifying the mission and mandate, and developing an operational strategy, was vital to create a sense of full ownership of the programme. The consultancy input in actual programming was largely facilitative, but Symacon also provided technical advice to ensure that viable plans were produced.

The second area of concern, organisational structure and systems, required a protracted interaction between consultants, the agency committee and staff.

The central problem identified in the diagnostic stage was the absence of a management structure designed to oversee the technical/service delivery operations. The process of creating this structure was characterised by acrimonious discussions. Elected officials of the BDA were suspicious that the process was intended to disempower them as the real owners of the BDA. They were fearful of being replaced by unelected members, put in place by the donor or the consultants, in a takeover of the agency by technocrats. This fear was strengthened by the fact that the people who would staff the technical structure would be well paid, while the elected officials were not.

In order to allay these suspicions, Symacon began an educational process for the leadership, justifying each post that was required, and carefully explaining the contribution of new staff to the work of the agency. Most significantly, BDA leaders needed to be reassured that technical staff would be subordinate to the political leadership of the agency. Winning the confidence of Board members to initiate these changes became the first sign of internal change in the organisation.

Symacon aimed to reinforce this trust and clearly specify the management and operational relationships between the two levels of the agency. The focus turned to developing accounting systems, human resource management systems, and refining day-to-day operating procedures. The consultants discussed BDA's information requirements for decision-making and operational control. Feedback from staff, plus Symacon's knowledge of system requirements in the relevant areas, became the inputs into the design of the accounting procedures, personnel policies and operations management procedures.

These systems were introduced in phases and submitted for discussion with both the technical staff and the leadership. Introducing these systems gradually gives time for staff to absorb and adopt them. The process takes a minimum of several months and often a year or more, and allows time for the agency staff and leadership to start climbing the learning curve. It also enables the organisation to adapt gradually and refine the systems as needed. Symacon scheduled many meetings with the Board to receive reports on operations and financial performance of the agency. These meetings were held four or six times per year. It rapidly became apparent that Board members were becoming more enlightened, more literate, firmer in their questioning, and were able to understand the technical reports they were receiving. Board development is vital as it builds the foundation for enhanced organisational and management capacity.

At this stage in the intervention, the panorama shifted as the donor suggested an expatriate volunteer to act in a management position. The rationale behind the proposal was that there were no skilled local staff to take up the job for the salary offered. The proposed solution was to have an understudy to learn from the volunteer. The offer of an expatriate staff member was accepted by the BDA, which felt that acquiring such a resource person would have an immediate, and positive impact. Symacon played an active role as intermediary between BDA and the donor and was involved in negotiating the type, duration and recruitment of the expatriate. Concurrently, other administrative and management staff were hired. Serious conflict emerged when a qualified and experienced administrator was hired to replace the chairman's son. A qualified bookkeeper was also hired.

After about 18 months, with staff in place and the increased competency of the Board evident, Symacon began to reduce the degree and intensity of support. An undeclared battle for supremacy then developed between the local consultants, the expatriate, the donor and the volunteer agency. While there was no longer a need for intensive input, it was felt necessary for the BDA still to have access to some ongoing support and assistance. The donor also wanted an alternative monitoring tool instead of relying completely on the BDA Board. As a result, an Advisory Committee was set up with representatives from relevant government departments, a local institute and Symacon.

The development of the Advisory Committee introduced further conflict into an already tense situation. BDA leaders resented this action, and felt that this signalled a lack of confidence by the donors. An undeclared battle for ween the local consultants and the expatriate, the main donor and the volunteer agency. The responsibility for convening the Advisory Committee meetings was given to the administrator of the BDA. Within half a year, after about two or three meetings, the staff was failing to provide adequate reports and other information required for monitoring purposes.

The Board failed to deal with the matter. They asked the Advisory Committee to address the problem. In order to avoid scrutiny and control, the administrator stopped convening the Advisory Committee meetings. Symacon was not in a position to interfere, and the donor did not want to be seen to be telling the BDA what to do. Thus the intervention ended. Shortly thereafter, the administrator was found to have been dishonest. He later fell ill and left the agency. In the midst of such turmoil, the understudy became frustrated and resigned, after two years of on the job training. BDA's deepening organisational crisis was exacerbated by a financial problems. Outside funding dried up, and many members using services on a credit basis failed to pay, generating a severe financial crisis. The agency has since continued to deteriorate. To date, the programme structure and strategies are in place, but funding has declined and staffing remains inadequate to carry out basic service delivery functions.

Lessons Learned

This case study illustrates that the provision of professional and skilled organisational development support is not sufficient to turn a fundamentally weak NGO into a strong and viable organisation. Despite two years of intensive support, the BDA leadership failed to take the initiative and adopt a more professional approach to its financial and organisational management. The input of the consultant is not the determining factor in an organisational development intervention. Positive change can only occur if the organisational space is given and there is commitment to change on the part of the leadership and staff of the agency.

Capacity building is a lengthy process. The process approach of intermittent consultancy is probably the most viable since it seeks to grow and nurture capacity in the agency. This process was also cost effective; it did not cost significantly more than a one time consultancy. This approach is also preferable because there was time to withdraw in between sessions and leave the agency to operate on its own. More importantly, Symacon notes, it led to the clear allegiance of the consultant with the agency. This differs from short-term consulting, where consultants do not have an opportunity to develop an affinity with the assisted agency.

A few conclusions can be drawn from this case study:

First, small enterprise development agencies uncomfortable with the notion of providing businesslike and financially sustainable services often run into trouble. BDA provides a classic case of confused objectives and a reluctance to adopt a businesslike approach to enterprise development. The BDA's ideological convictions were inconsistent with charging market prices for its services, and its concern for democratic decision-making resulted in unclear roles and responsibilities. These organisational and financial problems were compounded by its efforts to engage in a large number of activities.

This case illustrates the potential value of organisational development consultancies. In cases such as this, capacity building targeted exclusively at the programme, technical or administrative systems level would be fruitless in the long term. In these cases, organisational consultancy is required, in order to address the deeper issues of organisational culture, values and vision.

Second, donors are often required to initiate the process. It is often the case that the NGOs involved, caught up in day-to-day events, fail to recognise the depth of their own problem. In these cases, the donor can act as an external catalyst to get the process underway. While there are both positive and potentially negative effects of a donor taking a leading role in the capacity building process, in many cases, donors with an ongoing interest in the NGO performance are the entities which most readily perceive an approaching crisis.

Third, too many parties with a vested interest in managing the capacity building intervention can complicate the process. In the case of the BDA, there were numerous actors with a degree of vested interest in the capacity building intervention, from the donor, the volunteer agency, the expatriate volunteer and consultants, to the BDA staff and BDA members. Hidden agendas often complicate the process, with each of the key actors attempting to preserve their own interests. From the consultant's perspective, neither the agency nor the donor fulfilled its expected role, and Symacon was often placed in the uneasy role of mediating between the parties. In the case of the BDA, Symacon believes that if the process had not been complicated by a fourth dimension introduced by the donor (i.e., the volunteer agency), there might be sustainable capacity currently.

Different actors will have different reasons for being involved in the intervention, and their expectations should be made explicit. Even then, the consultant must remain attentive to possible hidden agendas.

Fourth, excessive donor intervention can disempower the recipient agency. The primary determining factor of a successful intervention is the commitment of the recipient NGO. Even with skilled and proficient consultants, the intervention is likely to fail if the NGO in question does not feel ownership of the process. From the response of the recipient agency at the end of the Symacon intervention, it appears that they felt many of these changes and decisions to have been imposed on them. This must be avoided at all costs, and the NGO in question must assume responsibility for its own decisions and institutional plans.

Fifth, volunteers need clear terms of reference and an understanding of their limited role. Introducing an external agent into an organisation can create additional stresses on an organisation. The role of volunteers should be primarily as educators, by transferring skills, rather than simply filling a position. This case is unusual in the degree of control which the volunteer sought to exercise, yet it does illustrate the potential dangers of direct intervention, particularly if the role of the volunteer is not clearly defined. It risks new forms of external dependency.

Sixth, long-term commitment to the process is essential. It is possible, given the fundamental weaknesses of the BDA, that additional support would have been useful during the change process. This was a disruptive period for the

BDA; new systems and procedures were being introduced, staff were being hired and fired, and programme contents were being revised. While keeping consultants involved for a longer period may entail the risk of dependency, it could be suggested that 18 months may have been an insufficient period of time for both a process of organisational analysis and change. Capacity building, and organisational development in particular, must be recognised as a slow and long-term process of change.

7.5 CONCLUSIONS: ORGANISATIONAL DEVELOPMENT FOR NGOS

Although there are common organisational challenges facing NGOs, successful capacity building must remain sensitive to the distinctive needs of an organisation and its mission, context, resources, and stage of development. The two cases presented here were of two small enterprise development agencies in different stages of their development, and which consequently had disparate organisational and management needs. The organisational development consultants, in these cases, tailored their approach to the needs of the individual agency involved. While both agencies faced structural management problems, underlying issues of vision and values were central to both cases.

The intensity of the consultant's intervention was largely dictated by the degree of organisational maturity of the NGO in question. A comparison of these dissimilar cases illustrates a few important points regarding effective organisational development interventions. Some of these are summarised in Box 7.2.

The Role of the Donor
The roles played by donors in the cases of the Triple Trust Organisation and the Budiriro Development Association fall at opposite ends of the spectrum. In the former case, donors were virtually excluded from input into the process, while in the latter, the donor was the driving force behind the intervention. From these cases, we can see both the positive roles donors can play in developing capacity building programmes for their Southern partners, and the dangers of excessive interference.

The Triple Trust Organisation's self-initiated and independent process of organisational development may offer a useful model for self-aware and relatively mature NGOs, both in the South and in the North. Donors were deliberately kept at a distance from the process, and their role was limited to an indirect one. Donors can assist such NGOs by facilitating access to the appropriate services and by being flexible in their funding and allowing for the costs of organisational development consultancies. Alternatively, Southern NGOs can categorise external consultancies as recurring operating costs, thereby spreading the cost between donors. This unconventional approach to seeking funding for capacity building may be suitable for NGOs that have a diversified base of funding. The more common scenario, however, is for donors to play the leading role in instigating the process and in determining the inputs to be provided. In the case of the BDA in Zimbabwe, this was conducted by a donor with which it had a long-standing relationship. However, we have seen that there are potential problems with this latter approach.

Donors have a vested interest in the capacity building of their partners, particularly if they have made funding available for that purpose. However, there is a danger that these services will become skewed towards the demands

---

Box 7.2 Characteristics of an Effective Organisational Development Process

- addresses organisation-wide issues, and does not diagnose a problem in isolation

- increases the ability of the organisation to address its own problems

- is facilitative rather than prescriptive

- recognises stakeholders and their agendas, and attempts to reconcile them

- remains sensitive to the cultural context and the existing organisational culture

- engages the support and trust of both management and staff

- ensures that the right to terminate the contract is held by the recipient NGO

- elicits perceptions at all levels of the organisations

- adapts to the stage of development of the NGO

- does not examine management processes in isolation from operational issues

- does not impose change

- does not unquestioningly advocate Western management structures and practices

---

of the donor, rather than of the client (Fowler *et al.* 1992). Moreover, there is a natural tendency for donors to prioritise those problems that impact most directly on them, such as financial reporting or proposal writing, rather than allowing the assessment process to define priorities. These problems can be avoided by having the donor cede control over the consultancy process, by providing the funds and enabling the NGO to select and hire its own consultants. The recipient NGO should retain control over the process and should be the sole actor able to terminate the contract if the consultant's performance is unsatisfactory. Allowing the NGO to oversee its own organisational development process contributes to the greater autonomy and self-reliance of the NGO, and ensures that consultancy organisations remain client-led.

Northern NGOs involved in organisational development interventions, or any other capacity building strategy, should ensure that the partner NGO has an active involvement in setting the agenda, establishing priorities and negotiating inputs.

The Role of the Consultant: Facilitative or Prescriptive?
In theory, organisational development consultants play a purely facilitative role. They merely assist an NGO to identify and explore options for improving organisational performance, and support the agency while it undergoes the turbulent period of implementing these changes. In practice, however, a more prescriptive role is often required. Consultants are then called upon to make concrete proposals in the areas of administrative and financial systems and organisational structures. The contrasting case studies discussed above demonstrate two NGOs which required different degrees of input from the consultants. In many cases, such as that of the BDA in Zimbabwe, a more directive force in the change process is required. Consultants need to be sensitive to the existing capacity of the NGO they are assisting, and adjust their input accordingly. There is a danger that a weak NGO will look to the consultants to make important decisions for them, and relinquish responsibility for their own decisions.

This chapter has argued that organisational development consultancy has great potential to make-long term and lasting improvements in organisational and programme performance. Yet, promising as this type of support may be, there is very little in the way of concrete evidence to demonstrate its ultimate impact. This is due in part to the difficulty of evaluating and measuring change, and establishing a causal link between an intervention and any subsequent changes in performance. On balance, however, preliminary experiences of organisational development suggest that it can be an effective way to assist NGOs to overcome organisational and managerial obstacles to improved and more efficient performance.

8
Strengthening Small Business Associations

8.1 INTRODUCTION

Donors wishing to support the small enterprise sector in developing countries can work in partnership with various types of local intermediary organisations. Despite their many strengths and comparative advantages, NGOs are neither the sole, nor necessarily the best performing, channel for small enterprise promotion. Among the most promising of local partners in the small enterprise sector are small business associations. These grassroots organisations, managed by small businessmen themselves, enable entrepreneurs to pool their human and financial resources and collectively access services that they would be unable to obtain individually. This participatory approach to designing and implementing support programmes makes associations highly attractive to donors seeking to build local capacity for enterprise promotion.

The dramatic upsurge in interest in small business associations in recent years reflects a growing desire of donors to contribute to increased social and political pluralism by stimulating the formation of organised groups at various levels throughout society. Small business associations are funded not only because of their service delivery capabilities, but also because a strong and mobilised small enterprise sector with the capacity to promote and defend its own interests is necessary for the sustainable development of the sector. By supporting small business associations, donors can encourage small-scale entrepreneurs to identify their own needs and to collaborate to meet these needs whenever possible.

Small business associations exist in many parts of the world and are varied in terms of their size, composition, purpose and functions. Their membership also varies widely and can be defined by trade, size of enterprise, or by locality. Many of the organisational problems faced by small business associations result from the difficulties inherent in managing a heterogenous membership organisation. The complexities of supporting grassroots organisations in developing countries have been discussed in-depth elsewhere (Gibson and Havers 1994, Levitsky 1993b, sahley 1995), and as have the roles and functions of small business associations (Levitsky 1994b). These authors have highlighted the importance of assisting and stimulating the self-sufficiency of these local organisations.

Associations play many important roles in the development of the small enterprise sector. They provide a forum for informal sector entrepreneurs to act collectively in both the political and economic spheres. Most associations perform a multitude of functions, ranging from advocacy and lobbying for favourable government policies, to the dissemination of information and education to members, and the provision of financial, training and marketing services. The roles that small business associations are best able to play, however, are still unclear and subject to debate. These multiple and complex roles are not always compatible within a single organisation, and the effectiveness of many associations is lessened by an excessive range of services and unclear objectives. The central problem facing many associations is the question of strategy and purpose. Most small business associations emerge to fill informal sector entrepreneurs' need for legitimate representation for negotiation with local or national government. This initial clear focus on advocacy is often diverted by the diversification of activities and the direct provision of services to members. The pressures for expanding activities are intense. Small business associations face pressure both from below, in the form of members' demands for more tangible benefits, and from within, for increased income to ensure financial viability.

Achieving financial self-sufficiency is problematic for associations. Membership dues invariably need to be supplemented with income from fees from the provision of services. Advocacy alone generally fails to generate the scale of membership necessary to make an association financially viable solely on the basis of membership dues. Despite the very real need of entrepreneurs for representation, advocacy is often insufficient to attract entrepreneurs as members. As pointed out by Olson (1965) in a classic study of collective action, potential members decide whether or not to join groups on the basis of an informal cost/benefit evaluation, in which the costs of dues and time expended are weighed against the potential gains. If costs appear to outweigh the immediate, tangible benefits of joining, potential members will decline to participate. The relevance of this to small business associations is clear. For the intangible activity of advocacy, entrepreneurs can reap the benefits of improved policies whether or not they join. For this reason, most associations are compelled to become involved in direct service provision to attract members and generate income.

Problems result when decisions to expand activities are made without reference to the capacity to deliver, or are made outside the association's mission and strategy. Examples abound of association. provide services which they lack the organisational capacity to do tively. This again raises the wider question of the strategic role of small business associations and their suitability as service providers. While there is considerable evidence that small business associations are able to become effective advocates for the informal sector, their performance as service providers is less impressive. Many associations, such as the BDA case study presented in the previous chapter, fall into the trap of trying to meet all of their members' needs, and end up failing to deliver any effective services at all. As specialist small enterprise development agencies, many associations feel obligated to meet as many of their members' needs as possible. These unrealistic expectations are often shared by members who place unreasonable demands on their association.

Where small business associations have been more effective is in establishing linkages with formal sector organisations. Rather than establishing their own service delivery capability, associations can access services from existing service providers, such as training centres, public sector organisations, libraries and information services, and even NGOs. In addition, there are some activities which associations may be well suited to sponsor. Entrepreneurs can use the administrative capacity of the association to coordinate joint activities, such as trade fairs or the development of databases of appropriate business information. Involvement in financial services, through rotating credit schemes or guarantee funds, is sometimes successful but is more risky and should be engaged in cautiously.

The relatively poor record of small business associations as service providers raises questions about their organisational capacities. They are plagued by problems of poor leadership and bad management, stemming from the voluntary and elected nature of these positions, which can be conducive to politicised and unprofessional management styles.

Small business associations are managed and operated by small businessmen themselves. Paradoxically, this is at once their most valued characteristic and the cause of many of their underlying problems. In the absence of sufficient income to hire professional staff to fill administrative and management functions, most duties are carried out by volunteer members. These entrepreneurs have the additional burdens of running their own enterprises and consequently have limited spare time available to devote to the association's activities. The absence of a professional management strata capable of running the association can seriously undermine its ability to function effectively. Additionally, these entrepreneurs, while having the skills to manage a small-scale enterprise successfully, are unlikely to have the very distinct skills need-

...rge organisation. It can be suggested that to ensure the ...ing of a large-scale, national association, an experienced core ...e staff is essential. Unfortunately this is subject to the availabil- ...ancial resources.

...related set of problems arises from the elected nature of leadership posi- ...ns which can lead associations to become politicised. As in politics, people are not elected to leadership posts for their management skills, but for their charisma and eloquence. Elected leaders also tend to be those with greater per- sonal contacts and a close following, rather than those with the capacity to advance the interests of members. In Africa, there is a culture conducive to authoritarian structures and organisations, and these patterns are often perpet- uated within membership organisations. Grassroots organisations are in dan- ger of coming under the control of a group or faction within an association. A Ghanaian consultant to the ASSI programme (see section 8.2) argues that in Ghana a mix of Western management and traditional structures is often used unsuccessfully. He argues:

> Most of the leaders of the small enterprise groups not only equate their positions to those of chiefs or queenmothers, but also induce the royal atmosphere around themselves. Against the spirit of the constitutions of the associations, the leaderships become inaccessible and unreplaceable. Safeguarding and perpetuation of one's positions take precedence over leadership's responsibilities and commitment to develop and maintain viable, cohesive, dynamic and sustainable groups. In some associations, it does not take much time for this misbehaviour to dampen the spirits of some active members thus introducing dissenting factions, passivity, power struggles, and even withdrawal of membership. (Amenuvor 1993:6)

These findings are not uncommon. In a study of small business associations in Africa and Asia, Gibson and Havers (1994) found considerable evidence of long-standing leaders and undemocratic practices, particularly rife in Africa. They suggest that rather than discussing at an abstract and theoretical level how democracy should be promoted in small business associations, it may be necessary to accept this as an entrenched feature of the African landscape. They conclude with a provocative question: to what extent does democracy matter, as long as the leadership is effective (1994:18)?

It is true that it is a Western bias to believe democracy to be the best way to select leaders. In fact, constantly changing leaders preempt the continuity which aids long-term strategic planning, as annual or bi-annual elections can be disruptive. It is also clear in many cases that members prefer the security

n a long standing leader provides. On the other ha...
e related issues of participation, representation and distri...
which are of significance and merit consideration.

Membership organisations in both the developed and developing...
have a tendency to become politicised. Groups of individuals with
interests may form cliques within the organisation, and may vie for power...
control over resources. A key aspect which potential donors must consider is
the impact of the existence of such factions on the distribution of benefits
throughout the group. It is essential that benefits, advantages and services
trickle down to the intended beneficiaries, i.e., the grassroots members. The
key distinction to make is that elitism in decision-making differs from elitism
and favouritism in control over resources and benefits. While the former
might be acceptable, the latter is not. Donors must be aware of the possibility
of the association being used as a vehicle for personal interests.

Problems surrounding the equitable distribution of benefits may also be
the unintentional consequence of poor management and of a leadership without a clear mandate from members. Small business associations claim to speak
on behalf of the small enterprise sector, and the ability of an association to
reflect accurately the interests it claims to represent needs to be questioned.
As with any organisation acting on a political level, there are difficulties in
representing a heterogenous constituency. The composition of the leadership
may (intentionally or unintentionally) reflect the interests of one group over
another. Potential donors should attempt to understand whose interests an
advocacy group advances in practice.

What can be done to ameliorate these problems? While issues of corruption and power struggles may be cultural factors which are difficult – if not
impossible – to remedy, questions of participation can be at least partially
addressed by modifying the organisational structure and implementing constitutional reform. Structural and constitutional policies which address the central issues of representation and participation in setting the agenda help to
minimise the extent of these dangers. If small business associations claim to
be speaking on behalf of a particular group, organisational structures must
enable members to articulate their interests to the leadership. Admittedly, a
constitution is no guarantee of democratic practices. But it can at least provide
internal mechanisms which guarantee members' rights and formalise members' inputs.

...e United Nations Economic Commission for Africa (UN-ECA) ...o a programme designed to encourage the small enterprise sector to ...estigate and develop proposals for the promotion of the informal sector in Ghana and the Ivory Coast. In Ghana, one of the outcomes of the year-long process was a decision by representatives of 32 business associations to establish an umbrella organisation unifying the multitude of existing associations. In response to these conclusions, the Association of Small Scale Industries (ASSI), has recently undergone a comprehensive reorganisation and redefinition of its roles in order to become an apex organisation for small business associations in Ghana. This case study of support for the ASSI illustrates many of the organisational problems faced by membership organisations, and examines how some of these can be addressed.

The Assessment Process

UN-ECA initiated a series of workshops in Ghana designed to explore issues surrounding the promotion of the informal sector and to develop recommendations for further action. Aiming to initiate a participatory process of discussion and debate, phase one of the programme comprised a series of workshops with representatives of 32 small business associations. This participatory workshop process was designed to assist the sector to identify its own problems and initiate actions to solve them. Informal sector entrepreneurs are themselves most aware of their needs, and according to the UN-ECA, they are, "the most competent to decide on what pertinent changes and reforms are required, and what new initiatives and actions are most needed for the good of the sector" (UN-ECA 1993a:2). The process itself was designed to empower the leadership of participating small enterprise associations by encouraging them to educate themselves regarding the problems the informal sector faces, raising their awareness, and mobilising them into action.

The director of the African Centre for Human Development, an Ghanaian NGO which offers training and consultancy services to grassroots organisations, was brought in as National Project Coordinator responsible for organising and coordinating the year-long process. Working groups were established to identify and define important constraints and to elaborate action plans to implement solutions to the most pressing problems. Working groups averaging fifteen members were formed to review the following topics as they relate to the small scale enterprise sector: government policy, finance, health and safety, education and training, and the networking and effectiveness of small business associations. These groups met on average sixteen times throughout the year, culminating in a national workshop in which working groups presented their findings and debated their action plans.

Among the most dynamic and stimulating of the working groups was the one that considered the effectiveness of Ghanaian small business associations in general, and the apex organisation, the Association of Small Scale Industry (ASSI), in particular. This case study will focus on the recommendations and follow-up activities of this working group charged with exploring options for strengthening associations.

Recommendations of the Small Business Associations Working Group

The small business associations working group had two primary focuses. It was, first, to discuss whether there was a need for better coordination and net-working among the multitude of existing small business associations; and second, to assess their effectiveness, and suggest how they could be strengthened.

There was a consensus that there was a need for an umbrella organisation to represent the small enterprise sector in negotiations with the government and to coordinate activities which would strengthen the informal sector. Without better coordination, they felt, efforts would remain widely dispersed as the activities of the many associations duplicated or contradicted each other. After considering a variety of alternatives, the working group suggested that the ASSI, whose constitution allowed associations as members, was properly placed to assume the role of a coordinating, federating body for the small business associations of Ghana. The working group decided to establish a capacity building programme featuring the development of an interim management committee to guide the ASSI through its period of restructuring and reorganisation.

The working group also sought to identify key management problems facing small business associations. In addition to the collective knowledge and experience of the participants of the working group who were each active members of a business association, the group engaged the services of a rural development consultant to collate their experiences and to prepare a study of the internal management problems of small business associations. According to the consultant, the underlying problem which continues to undermine the successful functioning of business associations in Ghana is their tendency to disregard existing constitutional principles or to fail to develop formal organisational structures. As a consequence of this tendency towards excessively powerful leaderships, members gradually disengage from participating in the association, leading to breakdown of communication and the ultimate stagnation of the association. In order to be democratic and effective, he emphasises the need to encourage a shift away from the concentration of power in the hands of the few towards one based on committee systems (Amenuvor 1993).

Organisational Constraints of the ASSI

The ASSI displayed many of the problems common to small business associations. Many of the difficulties it faced have their roots in its unclear mission when founded. The ASSI was founded by a group of dynamic micro-entrepreneurs who were brought together in a training course organised by The National Board for Small Scale Industry, a public sector body for the promotion of small enterprises. This contact acted as the catalyst by raising the awareness of these entrepreneurs regarding the many constraints facing small enterprises, and highlighting the advantages of collective action to confront them. The ASSI was subsequently founded in 1986 on the basis of the vague principles of mutual support and help. Unclear in its goals, it was unable to establish a focused and clearly defined programme. Moreover, its internal structure and poor management further impeded the development of a clear strategy. Its strategic confusion was evident in its membership structure which included both associations and individual members.

Following the recommendations of the working group, an interim management committee was created to guide the ASSI through a period of restructuring and reorganisation. The committee was comprised of prominent members of small business associations who agreed play an advisory role on a voluntary basis. The interim management committee attempted to identify the primary barriers to effective performance to be addressed by the reorganisation process[1].

The most salient problem facing the ASSI was its membership composition. The incongruous combination of individual entrepreneurs and sectoral associations as members allowed the Association to prolong its strategic indecisiveness, acting neither as an apex organisation nor a small business association. This structural problem was the clearest indication of the central underlying problem: an ill-defined focus, an unclear mission, and confused objectives. The interim committee, and the ASSI itself, accepted the recommendation of the working group that the ASSI should redefine its role as an apex association comprised solely of member organisations.

The ASSI also suffered from serious organisational flaws. Inadequate channels of communication meant that information was failing to trickle down through the sectoral associations to the base members. Communication is an essential component of an effective membership organisation in helping to maintain the interest and enthusiasm of members and keeping them informed of activities and events. Improving the dissemination of information and

---

[1]Personal interviews with Dotsie Kumordjie, Chairman of the ASSI Restructuring Committee; Wilbert Tengey, National Project Coordinator; and A. Sasu, President of the ASSI; August 1994, Accra, Ghana.

ensuring better two-way communication between members and leaders was deemed to be a vital part of the reorganisation of the ASSI.

There were also indications that members were becoming increasingly apathetic and disinterested in participating in the Association's activities. A declining proportion of members were paying their dues and this led the ASSI into recurring financial crises. This is in part the consequence of what Gibson and Havers (1994) refer to as the 'chicken and egg syndrome': the ASSI was unable to attract members because it provided few visible services, yet this lack of members meant that it was financially unable to develop new lines of programming. It is not uncommon in these instances for members to become disheartened and discouraged by the performance of the association. Thus the financial limitations on the ability to provide services can have serious consequences on the relationship between an association and its members. This was not only a problem facing the ASSI, but also those associations which were to join as members. The consultant engaged by the initial working group to study the characteristics of Ghanaian small business associations found that their inability to meet the demands of their members acts to reduce morale and solidarity. The resulting apathy and non-responsiveness of members can seriously undermine an association, particularly in periods of crisis (Amenuvor 1993).

Given these conditions, it is not surprising that the interim committee found decision-making to be restricted to a small elite within the ASSI. This concentration of power does not necessarily reflect the politicisation of the ASSI, but conversely, can be the result of the growing apathy of members. Evidence of this disillusionment of members was found in the conduct of yearly elections in which few members actively participated. This naturally results in a leadership with a limited mandate which may reflect the interests of one particular group or faction within the organisation.

Finally, the interim management committee felt that the leadership of the ASSI, while enthusiastic and well intentioned, had weak management and administrative skills. The small-scale entrepreneurs forming the leadership of the ASSI had no previous experience in managing an apex association, which entails such daunting tasks as balancing competing interests and managing conflict, coordinating a large number of sectoral associations with varying degrees of capacity, negotiating with donors, and organising elections. These problems were compounded by inadequate physical resources of the ASSI to maintain an association with national coverage. In particular, the absence of vehicles hampered the ability of headquarters staff to travel to the member associations and maintain close communication.

Despite these problems, the interim management committee was confident that the ASSI would be able to overcome these difficulties and become an effective coordinating body for the small enterprise sector. Its leadership was enthusiastic and committed to initiating a change process, while the trade associations that were to become members were eager to support and participate in the revitalisation of the ASSI.

The Reorganisation of the ASSI

The interim committee launched the reorganisation of the ASSI, and engaged the sponsorship of a foreign donor to finance the process. The focal point of the restructuring process was developing a more appropriate draft of the constitution. It was expected that a participatory process of drafting and approving a new constitution would strengthen the association by:

- compelling the association to reconsider its central mission and objectives

- engaging the commitment and participation of members in the debate by having voting delegates

- restructuring the membership and organisational structure to a more effective federated model

- defining the functions of district, regional, and national executive committees

- specifying and clarifying job descriptions for all management and administrative staff.

While the reorganisation was underway, a strategic planning committee was created to begin deliberating the vital issues of mission and objectives. Leaders from four prominent small business associations, who were expected to play a leading role within the ASSI at a later stage, were invited to join ASSI executives on the committee. It was clear that many of the functions which the ASSI traditionally played would have to be sacrificed in order for it to embrace the new challenge of becoming a federated body.

Processes of reorganisation and organisational change can be conflictual and disruptive. This study has argued that external guidance and facilitation can significantly ease the period of transition. External facilitators can play an important role in helping an organisation to identify options and in offering suggestions and advice for policy/programming changes. This external support does not necessarily take the form of local consultants as in the previous case studies. The formation of a committee comprised of representatives from other small business associations offered the ASSI a support group comprised of its peers. Involving the small business associations in the transition process also helped to ensure that changes accurately reflect the demands and needs of its constituency.

The strategic planning committee considered the role of the ASSI in light of the needs of the small enterprise sector and of existing small business associations. According to the draft constitution submitted for discussion, the primary role of the ASSI is to provide an "organisational framework for micro and small industries which will make it possible for them to organise and develop themselves" (UN-ECA 1993b:2). More specifically, the ASSI developed the following objectives:

- to be an advocate on behalf of micro and small enterprises and to oppose legislation which may have a detrimental impact on the sector

- to coordinate external collaboration for the micro and small enterprise sector.

- to provide a means for micro and small enterprises to articulate their interests

- to provide opportunities for training for entrepreneurs

- to commission or conduct studies which would benefit the sector

- to promote and ensure welfare facilities for members in order to enhance their well-being (UN-ECA 1993b:3).

The ASSI's newly defined objectives provided a basis upon which strategic plans could be developed.

The interim management committee also sought training for key personnel within the ASSI. Two donors were approached for capacity building inputs. One donor who had previously provided core funding organised a course on strategic planning skills for managers, while a second donor provided training in basic management skills.

The steering group also sought funding to obtain the physical resources needed to set up and maintain a secretariat. The proposal budgeted for a full-time Secretary General and supporting administrative staff, in addition to office expenses and capital equipment. Their rationale for seeking such funding was the need for a period of stability while the association consolidated itself. Once the organisational base was consolidated and activities were initiated, it was expected that the income from dues levied on sectoral associations would increase and begin to cover the operating costs. The proposal, to date, has not received funding.

The capacity building process of the ASSI is still in an incipient stage, and it is as yet too soon to see whether it will emerge as a strong and effective coordinating body for the informal sector. The reorganisation was merely the first step in what is likely to be a long-term process of organisational change and development. This combination of core funding, training inputs, and external support to help clarify mission and objectives, however, has been successful in helping the ASSI identify and confront many of the serious organisational weaknesses which have hampered its performance in the past. The support initiated by the UN-ECA has reached a stumbling block with the donor rejection of the core funding proposal. This apparent obstacle, however, may encourage the ASSI and its advisory committee to look beyond the physical and financial inputs and seek more coordinated and comprehensive capacity building support. It can be suggested that South-South linkages and staff exchanges with other successful and effective small business associations may be a more effective means of learning relevant management and administrative techniques than relying merely on management training and core funding.

Lessons Learned

This capacity building process provides a useful contrast to the cases presented in the previous chapter. The ASSI received a variety of inputs from different sources throughout its reorganisation period, rather than a discrete, defined package of services provided by a single donor. This has both positive and negative consequences.

The experience of the UN-ECA programme has shown that a donor can act effectively as a catalyst to a process of collaborative assessment and planning. In this case, it was not the donor(s) who established the direction and outcome of the programme. Instead, the committee of interested small businessmen, which had no donor representation, was primarily responsible for making plans and offering guidance to the ASSI. This process ensured that major decisions were made by the informal sector entrepreneurs themselves and were taken forward on their own initiative.

On the less positive side, donor commitment to taking the process beyond the assessment stage provides a degree of stability and security to those involved in the process. The UN-ECA support concluded at the stage where the working groups had developed strategic plans, and failed to fund a second implementing phase. Undergoing an assessment and planning stage may create heightened expectations and may ultimately lead to frustration if there is not some commitment to support subsequent capacity building efforts.

The case of the ASSI also illustrates a few important lessons regarding the needs of small business associations.

First, small business associations are often torn between remaining focused on advocacy and becoming involved in direct service provision. The ASSI illustrates a classic case of conceptual confusion regarding its role, and highlights the pressures placed on associations for the gradual expansion of activities and services. There are intense financial pressures on small business associations to engage in service provision, and it may not be feasible for an association to remain exclusively focused on advocacy. It should be noted, however, that there are alternatives to becoming directly involved in service provision to members. In Ghana, for example, there are associations that are primarily advocates and which supplement their income by collecting taxes from members for the government on a commission basis. This service to the government is also of benefit to members, who gain a degree of protection from harassment by government officials.

Second, small business associations need to be reminded that no single resource organisation can meet all of the varied needs of the small enterprise sector. Excessively ambitious goals are the downfall of many small business associations. Donors should encourage them to remain narrowly focused in their objectives in order to remain effective. According to Carroll (1992) the most effective membership organisations tend to be those that are narrowly focused and task specific. However, many donors interested in supporting small business associations tie funding to the expansion of programme activities. While associations can provide an alternative channel of service delivery to NGOs, donors need to be very cautious in encouraging them to become more heavily involved in training or financial activities. Small business associations need to consider where their comparative advantages may lie, and focus on those roles which they can best perform.

Third, there is a danger of excessive donor funding for successful and high profile associations. Donors and Northern NGOs are always looking for strong local partners with the potential for sustainability and good performance, and it is often the case that a handful of high profile organisations attract the attention of donors. In the case of the ASSI, inputs were provided by three donors, creating the risk of poorly coordinated inputs and capacity building strategies. More to the point, too many external inputs may suppress the organisation's spirit of self-sufficiency, especially if the funding provided is out of proportion to an association's own means. Gibson and Havers (1994) offer the commonsense guideline that funding be limited to 50% of an association's annual income. Unfortunately, as with the ASSI, the 50% mark is often greatly surpassed.

121

Fourth, a period of subsidy may be useful if the phasing out is planned at the outset. Core funding can provide the stability needed to begin new programmes and activities, and provide the basic physical resources needed for effective work. While this may provide the basis for an association to get on its feet and re-start programme activities, the danger of excessive financial intervention remains. Financial planning is important, and projections of income must be based on realistic calculations of the members' ability to pay. The case of the ASSI, as a federated body, is even more complex as its financial viability is dependent upon the ability of its member associations to pay their dues. Donors must be clear from the start about the duration of their intervention. If the financial support is for a limited period of time, an exit strategy which does not leave the association in a financially vulnerable position must be developed early on.

Fifth, in supporting small business associations, there continues to be a propensity towards financial and physical inputs in many capacity building programmes. A common pitfall, evident in the ASSI's funding proposal, is the tendency to believe that increased physical resources will lead to increased organisational capacity. Although management obstacles were identified as among the most significant constraints on the ASSI's ability to fulfil its role successfully, the proposal was biased towards hard, physical inputs, such as vehicles, computers, large offices, and core funding. Receiving considerable amounts of core funding for a limited period of time may only lead them to establish a secretariat which they would be unable to maintain and finance on their own.

Sixth, capacity building processes for small business associations must engage the participation of members, not just the leadership. Participatory processes of reforming and redefining objectives are particularly important for membership organisations. In contrast to organisational development support for NGOs, there is a large constituency which must be involved in formulating and approving changes. If members are not informed and consulted over changes relating to the direction of an organisation, the perception of imposed change can seriously damage morale.

Seventh, a clear distinction between the political leadership and programme managers should be made. Where income permits, the existence of paid administrative/technical staff (i.e., general manager) clearly distinct from elected positions (i.e., elected Board/President), helps maintain a democratic structure and a professional capacity to deliver services.

Eight, federating the multitude of existing organisations may be an important way to encourage the institutional development of the small enterprise promotion sector. A strong federation can provide information to sectoral associations and coordinate linkages between the sector and other actors, such as governments, donors, training centres, etc. Their large constituency gives them greater legitimacy in their negotiations with governments and provides a structure through which the small enterprise sector can speak collectively. A division of labour can develop between umbrella organisations and their member associations, with each playing distinct but complementary roles.

8.3 THE UGANDAN SMALL SCALE INDUSTRIES ASSOCIATION

Appropriate Technology Design and Development (APT) is a British NGO dedicated to the alleviation of poverty and the promotion of local economic growth in developing countries. Founded in 1984, APT works with in-country partners, including NGOs, small business associations and training institutes, to provide specialist support for small-scale enterprises. These agencies vary in the types of support programmes which they offer, and provide technical training, business training, credit, and/or the design and promotion of appropriate technologies for small industries.

Strengthening these local partners is a vital part of APT's strategy for sustainable small enterprise promotion. In 1990, APT responded to a request for support from the Uganda Small Scale Industries Association (USSIA). USSIA is a small business association with national coverage, with over 800 members spread throughout 28 of Uganda's 33 districts. USSIA has 8 zonal offices and a secretariat based in Kampala responsible for day-to-day management. Unlike ASSI in Ghana, it is an association solely comprised of individual entrepreneurs. It was founded in 1979 by 200 informal sector businessmen with the objective of becoming the primary representative of the small enterprise sector in negotiations with the government and other bodies. As with many associations, USSIA rapidly expanded into the provision of services to its members, focusing primarily on training.

In 1990, APT launched a three year programme with the dual aims of improving the effectiveness of USSIA's programmes, and strengthening its organisational capacities. This case study demonstrates a model of capacity building support in which the Northern NGO provides direct, on-site advice and assistance rather than seeking external sources of support, as in the previous case studies. This type of direct, partner-to-partner support is probably the most common model of capacity building.

Organisational Weaknesses of the USSIA

Organisational weaknesses were assessed informally during the project proposal preparation stage. Through a series of meetings and field visits, APT staff and USSIA executives came to mutual agreement regarding the priority issues facing the organisation and the nature of the support required. Throughout the lifetime of the project, APT staff were engaged in ongoing assessments and reviews of performance. With hindsight, APT recognises that a more thorough and systematic assessment process prior to the development of the programme would have helped them to design an effective intervention, as it later became clear that the organisational problems were more serious than initially apparent.

USSIA displayed some of the common functional problems of small business associations, many of which have already been discussed. Since its inception in 1979, USSIA had begun to show serious signs of organisational decline. Paid up membership was in decline, and basic administrative tasks were not being fulfilled. The following points are among the most serious problems identified by APT project staff in consultation with USSIA leaders.

The most obvious indication of the trend of organisational decline was the breakdown of basic constitutional functions and procedures. Annual general meetings were not held in the period between 1989 and 1992. In this same period, the board of directors failed to prepare accounts, few zonal elections had taken place and board committees had become inactive. Revitalising USSIA was essential if the programme was to succeed, and a cornerstone of this process had to be a renewed determination to adhere to constitutional procedures.

Additionally, lax management inhibited the development of an effective lobbying strategy or implementation an appropriate programme of services for members. Senior staff were not experienced in management and their inability to perform their functions effectively had negative repercussions throughout the organisation. APT recognised the need to develop a programme of human resource development which considered both the needs of the individual staff members and the overall requirements of the organisation. Many of the deeper management problems, however, were structural and could not be addressed merely through staff training. USSIA had become a top heavy and centralised organisation with a bureaucracy and administrative staff out of proportion to the needs of the organisation. It was imperative to pare down the organisation to a more streamlined and efficient administrative structure.

More significantly, the ability of USSIA to reach its neediest members and deliver appropriate services was in question. After an initial series of training courses offered to members, APT found that the centralised location and high costs of the course tended to favour better-off members. In order to ensure the accessibility of courses to grassroots members, USSIA needed to improve its capacity to target its services, decentralise geographically and develop more cost-effective courses. Providing low cost courses, however, can be a double-edged sword for many associations. They face the challenge of offering courses at a cost which most members are able to afford, while avoiding a degree of subsidy that might effect their overall financial position.

These organisational problems created the expected decline in membership and participation. With striking similarities to ASSI in Ghana, the percentage of members paying their yearly dues declined precipitously. In 1990, the year in which APT began working with the USSIA, only 73 of the 772 members paid their dues. It can be suggested that this decline was due in part to the limited concrete benefits felt by most members. This pattern, however, can instigate a vicious circle, with a financially insolvent organisation reducing the level of activities, only to lose more members and have its income further reduced. However, it should be noted that this drop in dues does not merely reflect the growing disinterest of the membership body, but may also indicate a moribund organisational structure which had become lax in collecting dues.

As with most small business associations, there were political overtones to these problems. USSIA had been characterised by increasing politicisation and internal factionalisation. As the organisation began to decline, the leadership lost the trust and confidence of members, while key staff became disillusioned with some of the elected leaders. However real the management weaknesses of the leaders may have been, there was a tendency within the organisation to place most of the blame on one or two key leaders. These personality conflicts may have served to mask the depth of the organisational constraints. There is a fairly common tendency within membership organisations to focus on the shortcomings of a few key individuals, thereby distracting both staff and members from recognising the organisation-wide problems.

The Ugandan Small Scale Industries Association
Faced with these serious structural, human and administrative flaws, APT initiated a three year process of support which combined ongoing advice and guidance, financial inputs, and training for key staff members. The APT support had two objectives: first, to strengthen the organisational capacity of USSIA, and second, to assess the needs of Ugandan small-scale enterprises, and to assist in the development of appropriate support programmes. Thus, the programming objectives were deeply interlinked with the organisational aspects, and the primary emphasis of APT's intervention was placed on improving the content and impact of USSIA's support programmes. The leading force in the capacity building process was the APT project director. His

extensive range of duties included offering technical advice, conducting surveys of members' needs, actively assisting in the development of training courses, and instigating USSIA linkages with other organisations. The project director was also to 'advise USSIA in administrational procedures and other aspects of its operation where improvements in the service which it provides may be made' (APT 1990:7). Thus, the primary capacity building input of the APT programme was in the form of a full-time project director who assessed, guided and advised the USSIA in all aspects of its organisation and programming. This continuous on-site advisory service provided a valuable source of support and guidance during the transitional period of organisational change and revitalisation.

The project began by surveying the training needs of members to gain essential baseline information and to obtain up-to-date information that would enable it to design programmes based on an understanding of members' needs and demands. A new series of training courses for small-scale entrepreneurs was initiated, in conjunction with the ILO programme, *Improve Your Business*. Alongside the revitalisation of the USSIA's training activities, APT focused on the training needs of staff and leaders.

Improving USSIA's management and administrative functions required upgrading the skills of staff at all levels in the organisation. Initially, some staff members were brought to the UK for training on fellowships, but this policy created conflict and competition among the staff. The perception of overseas training as a 'reward' for good behaviour is a common problem with both grassroots organisations and NGOs in the South. Subsequent training was conducted in- country or regionally when possible. Secretaries, for example, were sent to the Kenya Institute of Management to attend administrative courses, while other staff were trained locally. This lessened the divisive impact of the previous policy.

Specific activities were conducted jointly between the USSIA and APT. Successful lobbying requires a clear understanding of economic trends and their impact on the small enterprise sector. In order to provide a sound basis for lobbying and advocacy activities, APT implemented a research programme jointly with the USSIA to review government policy and assess its impact on entrepreneurs. Not only did this research programme provide the USSIA with increased legitimacy in its claims to represent the interests of the sector, but also provided an opportunity to learn by doing. Joint activities can be an effective tool for learning providing hands-on experience and an opportunity to observe and learn from a more experienced partner.

The project director also encouraged the USSIA to examine its organisational performance, and to adopt a more professional attitude towards its operations. Functional issues, such as preparing accounts and improving administrative procedures, were rapidly tackled. Administrative staff were also reduced in an effort to develop a leaner and streamlined secretariat. Real improvements were made in the management of day-to-day activities.

The project director also had to tackle the more delicate issues surrounding the role of senior leaders within the USSIA, and the poor relationship which had developed between them and members. There was a sense that leaders were not sufficiently concerned with the welfare of the grassroots members, who felt that the USSIA had fallen out of touch with their interests. Benefits and information were failing to filter down throughout the organisation, which necessarily led to declining confidence in the capabilities of the organisation. A growing recognition of these problems led to internal debates within the USSIA, which recognised that better communication and improved relations with its membership body were essential first steps. APT played an important role in stimulating and contributing to this debate. The director placed pressure on the Board to revive the annual general meeting which had not taken place since 1989. This restored the voice of the membership, and thereby enhanced the legitimacy of the organisation.

The project director's role as an external advisor was a difficult one. He had to strive to balance the desire for the USSIA to make decisions autonomously, with the apparent need to encourage proactively changes in policies and procedures. APT found that the USSIA was sensitive to external efforts to change its patterns of organisational behaviour, and APT was careful not to promote aggressively its advice on aspects of strategic planning or management. As the relationship between the APT project director and USSIA leadership evolved throughout the three year period, growing confidence and trust between them made the USSIA more receptive to APT's guidance and suggestions. As the project progressed, it was clear that the USSIA felt less threatened by this external intervention and began to value APT's advice. Sensitive issues pertaining to management or leadership problems were only openly discussed within the confines of a trusting relationship.

Preliminary Programme Outcomes
Improvements in organisational capacity are not easy to assess, and clear indicators can be difficult to develop. In the case of the USSIA, there are three major areas in which improvements can be seen: management and administration, legitimacy and mandate, and programme performance.

Visible improvements in the functional aspects of the USSIA's management were immediately apparent. The number of staff in the secretariat was reduced and the USSIA became more cost effective. While quantifiable indicators are lacking, APT points out that the USSIA is now capable of assuming basic management and constitutional functions with 'less hassle'. Accounts are now being prepared, board committees are functioning and elections are being held.

In addition to these organisational improvements, there are indications that the USSIA has become a more legitimate organisation with a mandate from its members. Increasing membership indicates that USSIA is providing a market-driven service which is valued by members. In addition, the proportion of members who are actively paying their dues has grown dramatically. APT also provided physical and financial inputs which enabled better infrastructure to be put in place, contributing to improved communication between headquarters, staff and members. Increased participation in USSIA events suggests that members have a renewed interest and confidence in their association. Additionally, recent elections brought into power a new group of leaders with a clear mandate from members. As a consequence of this combination of events, morale and a sense of solidarity is returning to the organisation.

Finally, and most importantly, there is an indication that USSIA is now performing better. An evaluation of USSIA's training programmes found that the enterprises owned by entrepreneurs who had attended courses grew faster than those who did not attend. Its ability to deliver services to those who need them most has improved. It is, of course, this latter point which is the ultimate objective of any capacity building intervention.

Lessons Learned

First, a systematic organisational assessment processes are the best short-term method of identifying weaknesses. In hindsight, APT acknowledges that there were many organisational weaknesses which were not readily apparent when the project started. The long-term nature of the support meant that these weaknesses did come to light in the course of the capacity building pro-gramme. It is preferable, however, to make a determined effort to identify the areas which need improvement at the start of any capacity building interven-tion. Organisational assessment tools can be an effective means of conducting a more formal and systematic assessment process prior to an intervention.

Second, this case provides yet more evidence to suggest that small business associations should remained focused on a few areas of programming. The efforts of APT to encourage the USSIA to operate and manage its own credit system were aborted after it became clear that the association lacked the capacity to implement such a programme. In contrast, its efforts to sponsor training courses, and engage the services of *Improve Your Business* to provide trainers has been very successful. The ability of associations to represent entrepreneurs and forge linkages with other support organisations should be utilised to its greatest advantage.

Third, capacity building processes are enhanced if there is long-term support which enables a solid relationship to develop. APT has now secured funds to extend this project and continue providing support to the USSIA. While concrete improvements have been made in the first phase of the programme, it is clear that the association could benefit from further support. Considerable time invested in the early stages of the programme was needed to gain the confidence of the USSIA. Long-term relations facilitate frank and honest discussions of sensitive issues, such as organisational weaknesses and communication problems.

Fourth, small business associations may require a degree of ongoing external financial support. Achieving financial sustainability on the basis of membership dues alone is a challenging goal, and may be one which is not realistic if an association seeks to develop various lines of programming. APT estimates that USSIA would require a membership body in excess of 3,000 to achieve financial independence. This target, which represents an increase of 200% over current membership figures, is possible in the long term, but requires increased organisational capacity in all areas to expand the programmes on a cost recovery basis. Northern NGOs and donors wishing to support small business associations need to have realistic expectations about what can be achieved in a short-term project timetable. The development of a small-scale, weak organisation into a strong nationally based service delivery mechanism takes considerable time. Donors and NGOs need to recognise the long term commitment required to strengthen the capacity of grassroots organisations.

8.4 CONCLUSIONS

Support for community-based organisations differs from traditional partner-to-partner support in that the capacity building inputs are not supplementary activities to project funding, but are the objective of the project itself. The USSIA, being a weak grassroots organisation rather than an equal co-implementing partner, required intense external intervention and support. While with well established NGOs, external facilitation is often indicated to avoid intervening in an autonomous partner organisation, direct ongoing intervention by a Northern NGO is often required for community-based organisations.

This chapter has merely touched the surface of the issues regarding the development of community-based organisations, such as small business associations. Capacity building programmes which have been successful with intermediary NGOs are not directly applicable to the context and needs of community groups. Community-based organisations have specific organisational needs, and capacity building support must be tailored to reflect those needs. Community-based organisations face the challenges of managing input from members, ensuring a democratic distribution of benefits, organising elections, and remaining closely in touch with members' interests. Moreover, in comparison with intermediary NGOs, they are likely to be comprised of staff with a lower level of education, or they may be staffed entirely by part time member volunteers.

There are two facets to improving the management capacity of community groups. First, there are the crucial issues surrounding leadership and group dynamics, including the distribution of benefits, conflict resolution, cohesion and solidarity. Second is the development of project management skills and improved ability to manage resources (Fowler *et al.* 1992:23). It is clear that these approaches are complementary rather than distinct; a management systems approach cannot be applied in isolation from group issues. The complexities of working with community-based organisations are such that they merit their own in-depth consideration and study.

As the needs of community-based organisations differ, so must the responses. NGOs must develop instruments for strengthening the capacity of community- based organisations which are appropriate to their stage of development. While some small business associations, such as those discussed here, have national coverage and seek to grow and consolidate a proper organisational structure, few associations will reach the stage of development where they require professional staff or formal management structures. It is the responsibility of the donor to provide an appropriate level of support and maintain realistic and modest objectives.

As these two cases illustrate, most small business associations could benefit from external support to help them focus their efforts more clearly. Strengthening the capacity of a community-based organisation requires ongoing support and advice rather than a short-term capacity building input. But as Esman and Uphoff note, this creates a 'paradox of assisted self-reliance', in which top down, external support is expected to stimulate bottom-up capacity and independence (1984:258). It is the task of external intervenors to stimulate the creation of local problem-solving skills and build on existing local capacity. This can only be done by avoiding the temptation to assume responsibility for decision making and planning.

The two cases discussed in this chapter illustrate two very different models and contents of external capacity building support. Neither case included an organisational development intervention, in the sense that there was no deeply engaged external facilitator leading the process. These programmes, nonetheless, did address management issues directly. Peer group support played an important role in the Ghana case, while direct intervention by the Northern partner NGO was the model in Uganda. The determinants of success or failure in these cases are quite different, in part arising from the nature of the external support provided.

The committee system set in place by the UN-ECA to guide and support the ASSI in Ghana has the clear advantage of being participatory. Ensuring that the constituency was represented on the committee which drafted the ASSI's new constitution and mission meant that the entrepreneurs themselves felt full ownership and responsibility for the process. Limited donor intervention in the decision-making process meant that the danger of dependency on outside actors was minimal. Yet, as Tengey (1993) notes, the committee system could have been made more effective with the support of an outside advisor. Time was wasted in meetings which were unclear and unfocused. More significantly, the absence of a facilitator or single donor led to a poorly planned process with uncoordinated inputs from various donors.

In contrast, donor influence in the APT case provided an overall guiding framework to the capacity building process. This long-term engagement by a single donor provides a much needed element of stability and continuity to the difficult transitional period. Yet, as Esman and Uphoff (1984) point out, too much direct assistance can lessen self-reliance rather than enhance it. This directive approach must be engaged in with caution and with sensitivity and flexibility with regard to the organisation's stage of development.

Operational issues were at the heart of the APT support. Understandably, Northern NGOs want to link capacity building directly to improved performance. With capacity building support in operational aspects of the USSIA, APT was able to generate immediate improvements in performance. Yet underlying organisational issues will need to be tackled in the years to come.

APT support leans towards the directive, rather than facilitative end of the spectrum, with more or less clear outputs expected. This approach is more common than organisational development consultancies, and has both advantages and disadvantages. Traditional partnership structures can be an effective means of comprehensive capacity building. However, as Northern NGOs get more involved in the internal affairs of their partners, they must consider their ability to provide management advice and consider the implications of intervening in their partner. These issues will be addressed in the final chapter.

9

Creating Local Credit Agencies

9.1 INTRODUCTION

Credit is arguably the most powerful tool for small enterprise development and consequently, is the input most often provided by NGOs to informal sector entrepreneurs. With a few notable exceptions, however, most micro-enterprise credit programmes have fared poorly in terms of scale, generally reaching only a few hundred or thousand beneficiaries. While effective in enhancing the income-earning opportunities of those reached, most credit programmes are seriously constrained by the capacities of their local implementing partners in the numbers of loans they can disburse and the loan fund sizes they can manage effectively.

In order to have an appreciable impact on poverty and the incomes of the poor in developing countries, NGOs need to develop models of credit delivery that enable them to reach vastly greater numbers of people. Given the absence of existing local partners with the potential capacity to establish large-scale, sustainable credit programmes, some official donors and Northern NGOs are seeking to create specialised credit organisations.

Many difficult questions are raised by attempts to create local organisational capacity from scratch. Can externally created institutions become viable and genuinely local organisations with African identity? Will financially sustainable credit programmes be able to evolve into sound and viable organisations? Although the issues of financial and organisational sustainability may be interlinked, they are distinct. NGOs and donors still have a tendency to assume that the former will automatically lead to the latter.

Arguments against establishing new organisations focus on the recent proliferation of indigenous NGOs in most countries. Direct intervention by Northern NGOs may inadvertently limit local capacity to implement small enterprise development programmes by bypassing local NGOs and poaching skilled local staff. Caution must be exercised in creating an externally initiated structure, whose sustainability may be tenuous.

The most persuasive argument for this approach, however, is that creating a specialist facility avoids having donors impose their agendas and priorities on existing NGOs. Many existing NGOs implement small-scale, income generating projects that are one component of a wider development programme. It may be easier – and more ethical – to establish a new credit organisation with clear objectives from the outset, than to encourage an existing NGO to change its policies and mission.

This chapter explores some of these issues by examining two contrasting approaches to creating local capacity for small enterprise development. The first case illustrates a transition from an Northern NGO micro-enterprise project, to an autonomous local organisation. This is not an uncommon trend. There have been cases of local agencies initiated as Northern NGO 'projects', created purely as a mechanism to deliver services to the target groups. As these projects evolve over time, they strive to increase their levels of cost-recovery and achieve sustainability. To avoid withdrawing abruptly and leaving a gap in the provision of services, some Northern NGOs set their sights on devolving to local control and encouraging the project to take on a life of its own as a permanent local organisation. Part of the problem these agencies face is the result of their histories as NGO 'projects'. The project mentality is hard to break, and subsidises once established prove difficult to withdraw. More important, becoming independent from its parent Northern NGO can create a crisis of identity.

One example of this gradual approach to creating a local credit agency is the case of *Bankin Raya Karkara (BRK)*. Established by CARE in Maradi, Niger, BRK is a minimalist credit programme that aims to become a fully independent, profit seeking credit institution within the five year life of the project. BRK has performed extremely well financially, and is currently recovering nearly 94% of its costs. The current challenge is for CARE's expatriate staff to exit successfully from the agency.

The second case study illustrates the distinctive approach of the Opportunity Network of agencies which specialise in instigating credit programmes. The Opportunity approach is one of a facilitator. It identifies local businessmen and bankers interested in establishing a credit programme, then leaves them to form a board of directors, establish statutes, and register as a trust. Only after a local organisation is established by those responsible for running it, does Opportunity provide grants for the loan fund. This process can take as long as two to five years. This method ensures local control from the outset and eliminates the need for a later, difficult transition.

It is hoped that this examination of these two very distinct approaches to developing local credit agencies will bring to light some of the key issues raised by NGO involvement in this field. Are NGOs the best agents to establish banks or bank-like structures? Can local institutions be externally initiated? Only honest and self-critical appraisal of our still elementary efforts at meeting the financial needs of the poor will shed light on these crucial questions.

9.2 BANKIN RAYA KARKARA RURAL CREDIT INSTITUTION: CARE, NIGER

Bankin Raya Karkara (BRK) is a minimalist credit programme which aims to become a fully sustainable, profit seeking credit organisation. This rural bank model was developed by CARE after three years of experimenting with a variety of support mechanisms for rural entrepreneurs in the Maradi district of Niger. BRK has since eliminated most of its support services and aspires to become a financially independent credit institution. BRK's programme methodology is geared solely towards reaching that goal, with no particular target groups or socially defined objectives. The medium-term objective is for CARE to withdraw, leaving the Maradi credit programme as a permanent and commercial credit institution in the form of a rural bank or credit association.

History and Objectives

In 1988, CARE initiated a comprehensive small enterprise development programme in Maradi, Niger. CARE experimented with a variety of support mechanisms for rural entrepreneurs, providing credit, training and appropriate technology to informal sector businesses in the region. This combination of services within one programme proved too ambitious. Although the credit aspect of the programme filled an obvious demand within the Maradi region, some of the other programme elements were less successful. After the first phase of the programme (1988-1991), CARE reassessed its objectives, and the range of activities was sharply curtailed in order to redirect resources into the programme areas with the greatest impact. The training programmes and credit programme were retained, but it was decided that these services should be operated by two distinct organisations.

The credit programme aimed to become a financially self-sufficient credit institution serving the rural population of the Maradi district. The conditions in Maradi were favourable for the establishment of a new financial institution. Maradi is the main business district in Niger and is home to a thriving informal sector. Despite the vibrant local economy, this area lacks any type of formal credit facilities. After the implementation of a structural adjustment programme in 1989, many of the national banks in Niger collapsed, leaving much of the country starved of capital. Although Maradi has been affected by the economic recession of the early 1990s, its local economy is bolstered by trade with neighbouring Nigeria. A lack of liquidity in the economy and the unmet demand for credit is particularly severe in rural areas, as demonstrated by the exorbitant rates of interest charged by local moneylenders. Despite charging between 200–1,000% interest on loans, moneylenders were unable to meet the local demand for credit.

These economic conditions underlined the need for a permanent and sustainable source of credit for the district, rather than a temporary inflow of aid which might disrupt existing economic systems. BRK was therefore conceived as a permanent credit institution that would inject and circulate fresh resources into the local economy, rather then as a temporary enterprise development project. Its goal is to improve the local economy generally.

BRK's Credit Programme
CARE rejected a 'blueprint' approach which would have brought a predetermined set of policies to the newly established credit facility. No prescribed set of regulations from the outset enabled staff and management to improve and adapt the programmes continually as they gained experience. The driving force guiding the development of policy has been the pursuit of full financial sustainability and improved financial performance.

As the programme has evolved over time, four distinctive characteristics contributing to the programme's financial success have emerged. These are: a decentralised distribution system, an unusually high degree of loan agent autonomy, demand-driven credit allocation policies and stringent default procedures.

The first important feature of the Maradi credit programme is its highly decentralised loan distribution structures and decision-making systems. Most aspects of loan assessment and management are dealt with by credit agents based in 13 regional offices, with the central office acting as a control and administrative centre. Although a team from the central office disburses loans, local branches are held fully accountable for loans issued by the credit officers in their region.

A second feature of the Maradi programme is the degree of autonomy given to loan agents with regard to their loan portfolio. The selection of clients, the conditions of loans, and the intensity of loan application assessment are left entirely to the agent's discretion. The caseloads carried by individual agents vary, with better performing agents able to handle over 1,000 borrowers. Linking agents' income to portfolio performance provides incentive for the responsible distribution of credit.

A third characteristic of the Maradi unusual for an NGO project, is its fully demand-driven credit allocation policy. CARE has neither targeted specific social groups, nor prioritised particular economic activities, preferring instead to establish a financial facility for the community as a whole. Emulating traditional banking practices, the sole criteria for loan selection is the client's creditworthiness and repayment ability. Loans are granted for any type of economic activity, including trading, production, household consumption, and even onward lending. Financial self-sufficiency is more readily achieved with scale, and policies which restrict access to a small segment of the community are unlikely to generate sufficient turnover to become financially viable. BRK's heavily diversified loan portfolio, both in terms of economic sectors and geographical regions, also has the additional benefit of reducing risk.

The fourth factor impacting positively on financial performance is BRK's willingness to enforce default policies, including the use of legal means. Tough collection policies give the programme a businesslike reputation and makes borrowers take their loan obligations seriously. The demonstration effect of taking repeated defaulters to court, seizing their assets, or in some cases, having them jailed, underscores BRK's seriousness regarding repayment and forewarns intentional defaulters.

The BRK loan fund was provided as a US$3,000,000 grant from CARE in 1988. Between 1988 and 1993, nearly 15,000 loans were disbursed, approximately 45% of these to women. The goal of BRK is clearly defined: genuine financial sustainability, enabling BRK to exist without external subsidies by generating sufficient income to cover costs, defaults and inflation. In addition to basic cost recovery, a measure of profitability is needed to accumulate savings which help manage long-term risk. BRK charges 12% interest – above commercial rates – in addition to a 6% administrative charge. By 1993, BRK had nearly reached the break-even point, including coverage of internaonal staff costs. Income generated covers approximately 94% of BRK's overhead costs.

The real challenge facing BRK, however, is not financial sustainability, which it has now nearly reached, but rather genuine organisational viability. BRK will only be viable in the long term if effective and capable management teams are developed and appropriate legal structures are put in place. The successful transition from a project both owned and operated by CARE, to a commercial Nigerien financial institution will be a difficult and challenging process.

Organisational Growth and Transition

The programme is now undergoing a transitional phase during which management positions are assumed by local staff. Local management teams are assuming decision-making roles and CARE expects to be able to adopt a purely advisory role in the future. During this transition, it is expected that local project staff will adapt and develop the institutional system (statutes, control-

136

ling boards, accounting systems) which CARE laid in place during the first phase of the programme. The central issues that will determine the success of the transition include the organisation's ability to procure skilled local staff, to develop of a genuinely local identity and to clarify the legal ownership structure.

BRK has demonstrated an extraordinary ability to manage growth and operate a larger loan fund size. The loan fund grew from US$3,000,000 to US$5,000,000 by 1993, making BRK the second largest bank in Niger. Streamlining and improving BRK's technical capacity was a central focus in this period. The relative success of this process is due to the flexible organisational design, which enabled operational and management systems to be continually revised and updated.

A decision was made to introduce computerised management information services to enhance financial accountability. Efficiently disbursing such sums required more sophisticated loan monitoring systems, and financial accounting processes. Designed to enable BRK's head office to track repayments and disbursements, and monitor the performance of loan agents, the rapid introduction of a complex computer system created many difficulties. Although these problems were short lived, BRK's director has suggested in retrospect that hand-entry accounting systems are adequate for most credit programmes. Introducing new systems too rapidly can stress organisational capacity, and the difficulties emerging in subsequent period of adjustment takes considerable time and effort to eventually iron out.

It is also clear that the degree of decentralisation established early on eased the growth process. A growing number of loan agencies were each fully responsible for their portfolios. The head office remained in control of administrative and oversight functions, but did not face the burden of disbursing a growing number of loans. A delicate balance must be achieved, however, between decentralisation and loan agent autonomy, on the one hand, and financial accountability on the other. Finding a structure that effectively decentralises decision-making without sacrificing accountability is a challenge facing all large-scale credit schemes.

BRK's clear mission and objectives also helped it to avoid many of the difficult strategic planning decisions facing most NGOs in periods of rapid growth. Traditional NGOs that are expanding their programmes are generally forced to reassess their social targeting practices, make strategic decisions regarding the allocation of resources, and re-evaluate their priorities and objectives. BRK's clear mission – disbursing the maximum amount of loans possible to the Maradi community – left little ambiguity as to planning priorities and programme aims.

A key determining factor in BRK's future success is not only the technical capacity of local staff but the wider more encompassing question of organisational capacity. The transition to local control is to be a gradual process, in which local staff must develop a feeling of ownership not only of its physical structures and policies, but also for its successes and failures. Flexibility is seen to be the key to this process. Rigidly applied structures and systems may prevent local managers from developing their own solutions to problems that arise. Only maximum staff participation in decision-making will foster a local identity clearly distinct from that of CARE. Systems and policies initially developed by BRK's expatriate managers will have to be modified and adapted on the initiative of local managers. During this period, CARE will be represented on the board of directors, and will hold the right of a final veto. This stage will be crucial as BRK becomes a locally driven institution, going through the business cycle and facing the problems and periodic crises which invariably arise.

Furthermore, in order for BRK to become an independent financial institution, important legal questions regarding the ownership of the loan fund must first be resolved. The issue of the legal structure and ownership has been the subject of much debate and discussion within CARE and amongst BRK's staff, a process made more complex by the lack of a clear legal framework in Niger.

After assessing a variety of options, such as establishing an NGO or bank, BRK is currently being developed into a credit association, which has the dual benefits of a wide membership/ownership base and flexibility under Nigerien law in establishing its own internal regulations. Procedures are being developed for establishing local boards to administer regional offices, a board of directors responsible for the institution as a whole, and a membership base. Membership will be available to borrowers who have successfully repaid two loans, and who are able to contribute a $50 membership fee. Members will comprise the majority of both the regional and main boards and will be given priority in the designation of future loans. It is hoped that by incorporating clients on the board of directors, an element of self-interest will be introduced into the system, ensuring that they remain dedicated to preserving the fund. A wide ownership base prevents the risk of control by a few individuals for their own purposes.

Lessons Learned

BRK provides an interesting case of a large-scale credit programme with good prospects for eventual financial and organisational sustainability. To date, the expatriate director has been withdrawn and a local director is now in place. Despite BRK's success in many areas, however, this transition process is not without its complications and difficulties. It is still too early to tell if BRK will survive successfully as a fully Nigerien financial institution. A few preliminary lessons, however, can be cautiously drawn from this case at this stage.

First, this case provides evidence to suggest that specialised credit institutions with clear objectives are better able to develop the rigorous financial systems needed for an efficient credit programme. The minimalist approach to credit distribution adopted by BRK has enabled it to approach financial viability. Cost- effectiveness has been achieved by processing a large number of loans and ensuring rapid turnover. In addition, intensive (and therefore costly) loan monitoring to assess the impact of loans on borrowers' standards of living has been rejected. If borrowers have successfully repaid their loans and second loans are requested, it is inferred that they have benefited. These streamlined, minimalist procedures that fail to evaluate the social development impact of the programme can be difficult for a generalist NGO to accept and adopt.

Second, even profit-oriented small enterprise development programmes can be effective in alleviating poverty. Although the extent of BRK's market-driven approach may sound severe for an NGO, it has been effective in reaching the poorest groups in society and enabling them to increase their incomes. Supporting economic activities can have clear social benefits, by improving living standards, increasing self-reliance and confidence, and generating employment. It is thought that BRK's policy of making credit widely available throughout the community helped to ameliorate the constraints on income earning opportunities imposed by a lack of liquidity in the local economy.

Third, technical assistance inputs need to be accompanied by more comprehensive organisational development support. Technical financial skills were imparted to BRK early on; now, wider organisational capacities need to be addressed. Technical proficiency, while essential for good programme performance, is not a sufficient precondition for sustainable organisational capacity.

Fourth, developing organisational capacity may require many years of support, joint control and finally gradual withdrawal. Abrupt withdrawal of CARE's support and crucial supervisory role could damage BRK's prospects for viability. NGOs sometimes remain tied to project funding schedules and often set unrealistic timetables for withdrawal. It is possible that Maradi, with an extended period of advisory support, will become a viable local organisation.

An exit strategy for the eventual withdrawal of external support, however, needs to be carefully planned in advance. Complex issues surrounding the transfer of assets and legal structure should preferably be addressed from the outset.

9.3 OPPORTUNITY NETWORK, ZIMBABWE

The Opportunity Trust, UK, is part of an international, Christian network of agencies. It joins Opportunity International, USA, and the Opportunity Foundation, Australia, in supporting 46 partner organisational in 24 developing countries. The objective of the Opportunity network of agencies (Opportunity) is to stimulate the development of small enterprise development agencies in developing countries. Over the past 20 years, Opportunity has developed an innovative approach to creating and supporting credit and training NGOs that are entirely staffed and operated by local managers. Opportunity aims to develop committed and genuinely local organisations able to become financially self-sufficient within an agreed timetable. The case of the Zambuko Trust in Zimbabwe illustrates Opportunity's approach to creating indigenous local partners. This case study illustrates the importance of fostering local identity and building organisational capacity while avoiding dependency on external support.

The Zambuko Trust: History and Objectives

The Opportunity network began its involvement in Zimbabwe in 1990. Its first task was to identify a group of successful businessmen and women wishing to assist micro-enterprises on a voluntary basis. Developing a strong and skilled board of directors is the central pillar of the Opportunity approach to partner formation. An effective board requires members that possess not only management, leadership and business capacities, but that also demonstrate the personal characteristics of integrity and motivation. The voluntary board should comprise a range of skills and experience, while providing a good ethnic and gender balance. Opportunity expects that potential board members should between them possess the following attributes:

- banking experience
- development knowledge
- professional representation
- community stature

- corporate responsibility
- enterprise experience
- government contacts
- spiritual conviction

The process of identifying committed local board members can be lengthy, usually taking months and many visits by Opportunity staff, but is seen to be the key to the long-term sustainability of the local organisation. The success of the Opportunity approach in attracting a high calibre of board members is demonstrated in the Zimbabwean case. Members of the Zambuko board include a merchant banker, an economist, an accountant and a marketing director of a holding company.

The first concrete task facing the Zambuko's board of directors was to register in Zimbabwe with the relevant government body as an NGO. The complicated legal process of registration challenged the board to function coherently and effectively as a group, not just as individuals. This task also allowed board members to demonstrate their competence and commitment. If difficulties emerge at this early stage, the option of modifying the board composition remains.

The second pivotal stage in Zambuko's formation was the process of defining and developing its mission statement. Opportunity organised an initial board retreat designed to encourage the board to formulate, in its own words, the objectives and purpose of the organisation. The vision of Zambuko, articulated by its board members, is of a nation where all people have the dignity of providing for themselves, their families and their communities. Its mission is to be a bridge for the underprivileged and to provide opportunities for enterprise and income generation. Encouraging the board to deliberate and define its mission is a key element of fostering local identity distinct from Opportunity.

With the mission and purpose clear, and the commitment of the board demonstrated, an intensive capacity building process begins. Opportunity's support was comprised of technical and organisational assistance, as well as South-South linkages (see Box 9.1.)

Opportunity was instrumental in helping Zambuko design and implement the operational systems for credit delivery. Recruiting staff was the first step. Opportunity's experience in other countries has found a competent executive director to be a key determining factor of success. Opportunity assisted the Zambuko board in defining the roles and responsibilities of the executive director. In 1991, after a lengthy recruitment process, the board appointed an executive director experienced in development finance who had previously served as Chairman of the Accounting Department at the University of Zimbabwe. The posts of Director of Finance and National Programme Manager were also filled by managers with considerable experience in the commercial and public sectors.

The director then appointed technical personnel, including finance controllers, credit managers, marketing and product development staff. As part of its technical assistance programme, Opportunity provided programme staff

Box 9.1 Opportunity Network: Capacity Building Inputs

- **Technical Assistance**
    - technical training for staff (in areas such as loan portfolio management, monitoring and evaluation, etc.)
    - loan monitoring software, and other technical resources
    - on-site technical advice on system development

- **Organisational Assistance**
    - facilitating mission workshop and subsequent board retreats to define goals
    - facilitating strategic planning sessions and encouraging the development of action plans
    - offering ongoing organisational advice (i.e., advice in developing human resource development plans and defining staff roles and responsibilities etc.)
    - organising ethics and values workshops with staff

- **South-South Linkages**
    - staff exchanges (executive directors to visit other programmes)
    - training for executive directors in the Philippines, with opportunities to meet counterparts in other organisations
    - Opportunity global conferences with all partner organisations

with training in the areas of credit distribution methodologies, loan portfolio monitoring, and accounting systems. Considerable emphasis also went into discussing the ethics and values behind the development of Zambuko, to help staff identify with the organisation.

At this stage, the technical assistance offered by the Opportunity regional office in Harare is critical. The staff of the office have considerable training experience related to both the technical aspects of credit delivery and wider management needs. A number of resources were made available to Zambuko, including a computerised Portfolio Management System, on-site advice, and financial support. Opportunity avoids imposing a single organisational blueprint on all partners, and assists the local organisation to develop the structures and systems most suited to its individual needs.

South-South exposure visits were a further component of Opportunity's capacity building support. The executive director was taken to visit established credit programmes in South Africa and Swaziland to increase his knowledge and awareness regarding methods of credit distribution. Observing a range of programmes developed their strategic capacity and helped them identify the methodology most suited to their local context. The executive director and credit officer were also sent to the network's training centre, Centre for Community Transformation, in Manila, Philippines. Here formal training was offered in financial management, programme design and implementation, and management. The executive director also spent time living with a poor family who has received a loan from a local Filipino partner.

Linkages with executive directors from other partner organisations is also an important component of Opportunity's capacity building support. Executive directors from other small enterprise development organisations in Jamaica and Kenya visited Zambuko, offering practical advice about the day-to-day challenges of running a credit programme. Opportunity also regularly holds international conferences where board and staff members from partner organisations throughout the world can come together and share experiences.

With staff and systems in place, Zambuko initiated a one-year pilot programme. Opportunity requires all of its partners to begin operations by implementing a small-scale credit programme to determine the feasibility of a larger programme. Only if the pilot programme is successful does Opportunity commit support to the partner with ongoing financial and capacity building assistance. If the pilot programme fails to perform as expected, both partners reserve the right to end the relationship. Zambuko's credit programme performed well, and Opportunity committed itself to providing capacity building and financial support for a five year period.

Organisational Challenges of Consolidation and Expansion

Zambuko launched its credit programme in February 1992 in the capital city of Harare and the nearby town of Chitungwiza. Later that year, Zambuko expanded its operations and opened a branch office in the rural village of Domboshawa. To date, Zambuko has made over 3,000 loans to small and micro-enterprises. Approximately 500,000 has been lent, with an average loan term of 7 months. The default rate in the first three years has remained under 3%.

The programme has expanded steadily since 1992 and performance indicators have been positive. Although full financial sustainability is not yet within Zambuko's grasp, it currently is recovering 60% of its operating costs, and three branches are fully sustainable. Throughout this period of growth and expansion, a few organisational challenges have emerged which Zambuko must tackle if it is to fulfil its goal of becoming an organisationally viable and financially sustainable credit agency.

First, maintaining board motivation and commitment is essential for continued growth and good performance. Board members are successful entrepreneurs in their own right and have either a full time job apart from Zambuko, or a business of their own. Some also sit on boards of other organisations. Given the constraints on their time, it is sometimes difficult to convene the board for meetings. Meetings are often postponed or face the danger of being poorly attended. Busy or distracted trustees with limited time to devote to the agency is one of the drawbacks of attracting influential and skilled board members. The benefits of having such a board, however, greatly outweigh the potential disadvantages.

The Opportunity Regional office in Harare sees as part of its role motivating and encouraging Zambuko board members to remain active and committed. Funding attendance at bi-annual Opportunity global conferences, for example, serves to provide additional incentive for board members to remain involved. However, as a local organisation, it will become genuinely sustainable only if it is assured of continued motivation without outside influence.

Second, Zambuko needs to define clearly the roles and responsibilities of the executive director and board. In the first years of Zambuko's operations, their distinct functions were not clearly understood by all parties. In many agencies, it is difficult for a board of directors to relinquish key decision-making functions and delegate responsibilities to the director. In the case of Zambuko, this element was further complicated by the fact that board members have more experience and are of a higher social and business status than the executive director. Early on, the executive director was inclined to accept board decisions without question even if he felt the decision to be inappropriate. A dominating board can inhibit effective hands-on management by the executive director.

Third, Zambuko has experienced difficulties in recruiting experienced financial management staff. Opportunity's staff personnel study of Zambuko revealed that proficient branch managers and good staff capacity at branch level are the key to successful operations. Proficient administrative staff at headquarters, while important, was not found to be as critical. The scarcity of skill financial managers and the salary that they can command, has made recruitment difficult. Zambuko also is concerned that staff will gain valuable financial management experience and then flee to higher paying jobs in the commercial sector. Enterprise development NGOs must guard against becoming free training schools for the commercial finance sector. Despite this threat, to date, only one Zambuko staff member has left to join another agency. Staff departure is avoided by careful salary scaling, and attempts to nurture a sense of organisational identity and commitment to this Christian NGO.

Other staff and human resource development problems are emerging as a result from programme expansion. Each position is expanding in scale and in scope, so the problem lies in upgrading skills to keep pace with growing responsibilities.

Fourth, as the programme expands, it has become evident that there is an overcentralisation of programme activities and management functions in the head office. Zambuko is presently operating in four regions and plans to expand to nine regions by 1997. In order to develop the logistical and organisational capacity to create new branches throughout the country, Zambuko will need not only to decentralise its operational structure, but develop new management systems that ensure accountability and flexibility.

The Way Forward

The Opportunity regional office in Harare provides management advice and technical support to the Zambuko Trust. Regional staff offer guidance to the executive director and board throughout the strategic and organisational planning process. Zambuko and Opportunity are jointly attempting to tackle the organisational constraints discussed above.

First, efforts are being made to clarify and redefine role of executive director and the board of directors. Opportunity's regional director has encouraged the organisation to clarify and formalise board decision-making processes. In particular, it was important to stress the difference between formal board decisions and the instructions of individual board members which the executive director had previously felt bound to carry out. It was also decided that the executive director should play the role of chief policy advisor to the board of directors. Board members have been encouraged to recognise the superior and in-depth knowledge of the executive director on Zambuko's day-to-day operations and involve him in strategic decision making.

It is also important to note that as the agency goes through different stages of development, the role of the board and executive director change. In the first years, their roles were more operational and direct involvement, particularly of the executive director, was required. The executive director ran the loan portfolio, wrote monthly financial reports, and prepared reports and proposals for donors. Now his role is more strategic in nature, involving long-term planning, overall management, financial oversight and relations with the board.

Secondly, Zambuko has also decided to revise its organisational structure in anticipation of continued programme expansion. A key element of equipping Zambuko with the organisational capacity for national coverage is a more decentralised structure with greater branch autonomy and the reduced involvement of the head office in day-to-day operations. New branch offices are planned, and each will be responsible for its own loan portfolios.

It is not only financial responsibility that must be decentralised, but also management and decision-making functions. Zambuko is currently developing plans to restructure the board so that there are representatives in each region. Regional boards of directors will be created, with the chairman of each joining the national board. It is envisaged that by 1996 with five branch offices functioning, the national board of directors will have 15–20 members and the total membership of the regional boards will be 20–25.

Third, as loan officers handle more loans and branch managers become responsible for larger loan funds, recruitment and training policies must keep pace with these demands. Zambuko's human resource development plan seeks to ensure that the skills of staff are continuously upgraded to suit the requirements of the agency. In addition, Opportunity continues to provide staff training on technical issues.

Fourth, both Opportunity and Zambuko continue in their efforts to nurture and foster a sense of shared vision and identity throughout all levels of the organisation. Arguably, this is particularly important for an externally initiated agency such as Zambuko. To avoid potential problem of dependency and confused identity, considerable effort is being made to nurture a sense of staff commitment. This is done in part through retreats and staff attendance at regional and international training centres.

Lessons Learned

Zambuko Trust is an Zimbabwean organisation with full legal autonomy from the Opportunity network of agencies. Although it continues to receive financial and advisory support from Opportunity, its registration as an NGO has enabled it to forge relationships with other foreign donors. The prospects for its organisational sustainability without Opportunity's support appear strong. This case illustrates a few important lessons:

First, building organisational capacity requires a long term commitment. In the Opportunity approach, capacity building is not seen as a temporary intervention or based on a package of technical inputs. Increased organisational capacity is seen as the long-term outcome of an ongoing partnership. A complex mix and correct sequencing of assistance inputs appropriate to an organisation's stage of development is required over a period of years. Additionally, in order to meet the needs of its local partners, Opportunity's field offices are designed almost exclusively to provide organisational and technical capacity building support.

Second, in order to foster local identity and capacity, direct external involvement should be minimised. Opportunity seeks to be a catalyst that sparks local businessmen and women to establish a local NGO. No expatriate staff are ever posted in the partner organisations and the local boards are fully responsible for registering the agency as a local NGO. The Opportunity regional office attempts to minimise its interference and avoids being prescriptive in order not to inhibit the problem solving capacity of local management. This facilitative approach, however, can be difficult to maintain in practice. Problems have been experienced by Opportunity in other countries where the cultural norms of deference to authority has meant that some local partners have felt obliged to heed Opportunity's advice. In the case of Zambuko, however, there appears to be a healthy relationship in which the executive director and board feel free to express disagreements with Opportunity's regional staff.

Third, a local identity needs to be actively cultivated. Opportunity feels that the development of the agency's mission by the local board is a key step to developing a clear organisational identity. This compels the board to articulate its own vision and objectives without external intervention. Developing a strong sense of staff commitment is also an explicit objective of Zambuko's human resource development plan.

Fourth, capacity should be demonstrated before substantial funding is offered. Opportunity's approach prioritises capacity first, with funding later. Board members are required to demonstrate their commitment and competence prior to engaging Opportunity's support for the pilot project. Additionally, no long-term commitment is made until the one-year pilot has been successfully completed.

Fifth, the possibility of failure must be acknowledged and provisions made for this eventuality. The Opportunity approach allows for a reassessment and possible exit after a one-year period. In some instances, Opportunity has discontinued the relationship after the pilot project. NGOs seeking to create new organisations must avoid the tendency when confronted with weakness to redouble efforts and concentrate resources on an organisation with limited potential for viability.

9.4 CONCLUSIONS

This study has argued that Northern NGOs should work with Southern partner organisations, (either NGOs or CBOs) to build sustainable local capacity for social and economic development. In many cases, however, NGOs are working in regions where appropriate local structures for enterprise development are lacking. Given the absence of potential partners in many parts of Africa, Northern NGOs have no option but to create a new enterprise development organisation. In places where credit agencies are unlikely to emerge spontaneously, donor initiated programmes may be the only opportunity for informal sector businesses to access credit.

The distinct approaches of CARE and the Opportunity network of agencies considered in this chapter do not merely reflect different development paradigms and beliefs, but are conditioned by the opportunities and constraints of their local environment. The facilitative approach of the Opportunity Trust, while preferable for the reasons discussed earlier, is not a viable strategy in all local contexts. Although in urban areas, such as Harare, Opportunity could draw on the skills of motivated businessmen willing to dedicate time to establish a credit programme, in rural areas such as Maradi, conditions are not conducive to the establishment of a local agency. In order to meet the financial needs of the rural poor in the Maradi region where few formal structures of any kind exist, CARE had to engage in the direct provision of services.

Building an organisation from the ground up is a task fraught with difficulties. Externally instigated organisations are vulnerable to collapse after the withdrawal of outside support. An inadequate or poorly planned exit strategy results in local managers suddenly being asked to assume responsibilities for which they are poorly prepared. In the case of BRK, gradual, phasing out of direct intervention with CARE continuing to play a purely advisory role, has been proposed to minimise the disruption to the agency. However, there is no guarantee that local management teams will be able to maintain BRK as a viable credit institution in the long term. The success of this transition will depend largely on the initiative and capacity of local managers and staff.

The Opportunity approach recognises the frailty of new organisations and acknowledges the possibility of failure. Opportunity allows weak projects to collapse before funds are committed, not after years of support. The approach challenges local boards to demonstrate capacity first, with grants made only after minimum standards have been reached.

Zambuko's efforts to achieve financial sustainability are more long-term than BRK's. Its status as a local NGO means that it can receive grants from other sources. Local organisational control does not necessarily require full financial independence from Northern funding. The less ambitious aims of the Zambuko Trust in the short-term may be more readily achieved than BRK's goal of self-sufficiency without any form of external funding.

Part Five

Conclusions

10

Strengthening the Capacity of Southern NGOs: Going Beyond the Rhetoric of Partnership

10.1 INTRODUCTION

The current interest in capacity building and institutional development reflects the changing conceptualisation of the role of external assistance in third world development. Earlier aid strategies were founded on the belief that underdevelopment could be addressed by filling the technological and financial gaps present in underdeveloped societies. Technological and financial gaps are indeed significant, but in the long term, it is the ability to use these resources productively that is essential for development. As NGO strategies became more sophisticated and less welfare-oriented, they have placed greater emphasis on encouraging local initiative and developing local skills. Building local capacity for social and economic development, rather than merely transferring resources, is now recognised as the key to sustainable development.

This study focused on capacity building methods for intermediaries in third world development, such as NGOs and small business associations. It has emphasised that capacity building is not merely a tool to improve the performance of local organisations, but is part of a new generation of NGO strategies concerned with wider processes of institutional development. NGOs are recognising that fully functioning economies and societies require strong and effective organisations throughout society, ranging from the state and public sector, to the private sector, the non-profit sector and, finally, the grassroots level. Organised groups throughout society contribute to increased social and political pluralism, increasing the ability of the population to act collectively and express their interests to policymakers. Strengthening groups in civil society can lead to greater participation in decision-making and in the allocation of resources. In addition to strong organisations, good governance, and positive policy and legislative frameworks are a fundamental part of this process approach to development.

Development can no longer be defined purely in economic terms. Experience has shown that countries can grow in macro-economic terms, but economic growth can also give rise to greater inequalities, growing bureaucracy and increasing graft and corruption. Development is essentially about enabling third world countries to develop the skills, capacities and institutions which allow them to assume control over the direction of their development. Strengthening local capacity to use available human, financial and technological resources in a productive and equitable way is the ultimate goal of any capacity building or institutional development intervention.

It is important for NGOs to understand the distinction and relation between organisational development and institutional development. Capacity building and organisational development of individual local partners is merely one component of a wider process of empowering Southern NGOs and encouraging the development of a strong and autonomous sector.

10.2 KEY ISSUES IN SUCCESSFUL CAPACITY BUILDING FOR SOUTHERN NGOs

Capacity building inputs cannot be narrowly defined. In practice, capacity building can include any combination of a number of inputs designed to assist an NGO to become stronger, more effective and autonomous. As the case studies in the book illustrate, the depth and composition of programmes vary widely. These can range from a single, short-term input to address a specific problem to a deeply engaged process of organisational change and improvement. In addition, there are diverse sources of capacity building support. Northern NGOs can hire specialist consultants (e.g. Symacon in Zimbabwe), instigate and fund a process of self-assessment (e.g. ASSI in Ghana), or directly implement a process of deep engagement in a partner organisation (e.g. APT in Uganda). Northern NGOs can also play a purely supportive, funding role to a partner wishing to retain control of the organisational development process, as in the case of the Triple Trust Organisation in South Africa.

NGOs must adopt a pragmatic approach to capacity building by carefully tailoring support and assistance to the needs of each partner. It is unlikely that a blueprint package of services can be developed and applied uniformly to several of an agency's partners. Similar agencies can have dissimilar needs, and Northern NGOs must find the right combination and timing of inputs to suit the needs of each partner. The nature of the intervention will depend on many variables such as the stage of development of the local organisation, the source of its organisational problems, and its organisational culture. Capacity building support, moreover, will need to be continuously adapted and refined as the intervention progresses.

The case studies presented in earlier chapters illustrate the wide range of capacity building approaches which Northern NGOs and donors are developing. These differed in many key areas, such as the nature of organisational problems involved, the content of the capacity building support, and the role of donors. Despite the disparate nature of these case studies, there are common characteristics of successful interventions that can be highlighted.

The Importance of Organisational Assessment

If capacity building interventions are to have a real impact on organisation-wide capacities, they must be based on a genuine understanding of the organisational culture and weaknesses of the partner NGO. Capacity building should be prefaced by systematic assessment to identify existing strengths and weaknesses and provide an understanding of organisational and administrative practices. The value of an in-depth assessment is exemplified by the case of the BDA in Zimbabwe. Prior to the intervention, the organisational development consultants, Symacon, spent considerable time observing and understanding the internal daily operations of the client agency. This information enabled the consultants to participate fully and knowledgeably in the process of reforming policy and procedures. Similarly, the lengthy process of self-assessment initiated by the Triple Trust Organisation enabled it to design a sound and appropriate plan of organisational development.

Despite the clear benefits of systematic organisational assessment, in the vast majority of cases the areas targeted for improvement are identified informally by the donor agency. This type of 'assessment from above' on the basis of incomplete information can lead to inappropriate and potentially harmful interventions. Informal assessments often lead to the identification of vague and overgeneralised areas for improvement, and can pre-empt the specific targeting of problems. The generic solutions to oversimplified problems that result are largely ineffective.

Organisational assessment, however, is neither simple nor straightforward. The methodology used for assessment will determine its effectiveness. It is essential, for example, to use a consultative and participatory approach to ensure that real, rather than perceived, needs are addressed. Northern NGOs tend to prioritise those shortcomings that are most apparent to them, such as poor proposal writing or weak financial accounting skills. The management and board of the partner NGO, similarly, may be more concerned with fund raising issues than with issues of participation or staff-management relations. It is essential that both parties set aside preconceived notions of what is needed and allow the organisational assessment process to dictate capacity building priorities. An effective organisational assessment process allows the partner the opportunity to set its own priorities with the full participation of staff, culminating in the establishment of clear targets and goals for improvement.

As with the capacity building intervention itself, the leading actor in the assessment process can vary. As these case studies show, assessments can be externally facilitated, as in the case of the BDA in Zimbabwe; internally initiated and led, as conducted by the Triple Trust in South Africa; or conducted by the Northern NGO, as with the USSIA in Uganda. An in-depth assessment implies a significant investment in time and resources, and will require up to a few months of deep engagement with the partner NGO.

Cost considerations often lead NGOs to shy away from hiring consultants who are skilled in facilitating assessment processes. The benefits of an in-depth assessment are reaped immediately during the capacity building stage, by ensuring that the resources invested in the intervention are appropriately targeted. Investing in organisational assessment pays off. It should be pointed out that for funding purposes, this can be built into the capacity building process as a necessary first phase, rather than part of pre-programme planning. For example, a two-year project budget can include a 3-month assessment stage, followed by a 21-month intervention.

Organisational assessment frameworks which identify key organisational capacities and suggest indicators are becoming available. The use of these frameworks can provide a better understanding of the values, mission, and capacities of Southern NGOs leading to deeper and enriched partnerships.

Relating Technical Support to Organisational Capacity

Although this study has emphasised the importance of organisational aspects of capacity building, this does not diminish the usefulness of technical support for NGOs. Technical and project-related support can make immediate improvements by removing operational barriers to enhanced performance. Most small enterprise development agencies could benefit from outside input in areas such as establishing financial accounting procedures, improving client monitoring systems, streamlining loan assessment policies and fixing interest rates at a level which will contribute to financial viability.

Most capacity building programmes continue to have an operational, product delivery focus. Northern NGOs and donors need to relate the provision of technical resources to the ability of the recipient agency to use these resources. It is increased organisational capacity to use resources which provides a solid foundation for technical improvements. Merely providing assistance in the product delivery areas of an organisation can fail to address the deeper underlying capacities which organisations need to be effective. Technical support in isolation may be effective in solving particular problems, but may make a more limited contribution to organisational strengthening and maturity.

Continuing to provide technological and financial resources to weak organisations, moreover, can become a constant drain on limited aid resources. To adapt an analogy from James (1994b), donors can continue to pour money into a bottomless pit by continuing to provide resources to weak NGOs. To be more effective, however, efforts must first be made to seal the pit through capacity building interventions.

NGOs now recognise the importance of good management for project performance. However, the development of management theories and models appropriate for NGOs is still at a preliminary stage. Furthermore, there is a need for commercial management models to be adapted, not only for the NGO sector, but to specific cultural contexts.

Source of Initiative and Ownership

A number of variables determine the impact of a capacity building programme, including the skills of the facilitator, the effectiveness of the organisational assessment process in setting achievable and appropriate priorities, and the quality of the inputs provided. Most significant of these is the motivation and commitment of the recipient NGO. Capacity building support cannot be imposed. An NGO which has itself initiated the process will be more receptive to advice and willing to embrace change.

Although local initiative is preferable, many weaker NGOs will need an external catalyst to encourage them to recognise and address their organisational problems. But while the source of initiative may be external, such as in the case of the Budiriro Development Agency and the Zambuko Trust in Zimbabwe, it is essential that the local agency feels a sense of ownership and control over the process. In the case of the Zambuko Trust, considerable efforts were made by the Opportunity Network to ensure that the process of instigating and developing local capacity for enterprise development was led by the local management team, and not imposed from above. In the case of the BDA, this local sense of ownership was not actively cultivated and the intervention suffered as a result.

Terms and conditions must be designed to give the client the maximum control possible. It is preferable for Northern donors to provide funds for partners to hire organisational development or training services, rather than directly hiring the services. Allowing partners to choose the service provider not only ensures that suppliers remain market-driven to the needs of clients rather than funders, but also increases the commitment of the client to make best use of the services. If consultants are to play a leading role in an organisational development process, donors should relinquish control over the process, and allow the consultants to report to the client. Having consultants report back to the donors can have a damaging effect by encouraging the partner to minimise organisational problems rather than being open and honest.

Depth of Engagement

Many Northern NGOs engaged in capacity building have unrealistic expectations of the depth of organisational change and improvement which can be achieved in a limited, project-based time period. While technical capacity building inputs may achieve visible improvements in the short term, interventions seeking to have wider organisational impact will necessarily require a more serious commitment from both donor and recipient NGOs.

It is relatively easy to transfer knowledge and skills to an organisation. To begin to change attitudes, individual and organisational behaviour, however, is more difficult, requiring substantial investment in time and greater frequency of contact. For these reasons, organisational development should be conceived as a long-term, continuous process which is a cornerstone of an ongoing partnership. Instead of viewing 'capacity building' as a specific, short-term input, organisational advice, training and consultancy can be offered over a period of years as part of a supportive relationship between Northern and Southern NGOs.

The aim of organisational development support should be to encourage planned change and growth. These case studies have shown that organisational change in many NGOs is in response to immediate needs and crises. NGOs ought to replace a reactive approach to developing management systems and policies with a long-term plan for organisational growth and development. A long-term and continuous support process can help an NGO develop a planning approach to its own organisational development.

Sensitive organisational issues, moreover, are more effectively addressed within the context of an existing relationship. As the case of the USSIA in Uganda illustrates, many key issues were able to be addressed only after a period of years during which APT and USSIA had developed a close and trusting relationship.

Not all Northern NGOs are willing or able to become deeply engaged in capacity building for their partners. For those agencies which do not foresee long term relationships extending beyond the project cycle, it should be stressed that short-term inputs, such as training, do have an important role to play. For all of its organisational limitations, training can develop the individual skills which provide the foundation for wider organisational improvements. Southern NGOs should be encouraged to identify their own training needs, and turn to their Northern partners for financial support to meet them. Northern NGOs providing short-term assistance and inputs should do so with an awareness of the wider organisational issues and processes highlighted in the case studies.

The Need for Evaluation

Management capacity building and organisational development for NGOs is a relatively new field. The embryonic nature of this work is evident in the absence of tried and tested evaluation tools and indicators in the field. While increasing amounts of funding are being channelled towards capacity building programmes, there is limited feedback regarding the relative success of the various approaches. One difficulty in evaluating capacity building interventions is that benefits are long term and are not easily quantifiable. It can also be difficult to establish a clear causal link between the intervention and subsequent changes in organisational performance. The challenge facing practitioners and advocates in the capacity building field is to develop tools for evaluating the impact and effectiveness of interventions. In the absence of clear evidence that such investments offer a worthwhile return, donors will understandably remain wary of increasing funding for these programmes.

This study has argued that organisational assessment processes should culminate in the development of quantifiable indicators to provide essential baseline information from which change can be measured. Indicators also establish clear targets for improvement. Unfortunately, most capacity building process fail to do so and the case studies presented in earlier chapters are no exception. A concise list of quantifiable indicators drawn up to assess the impact of the intervention on organisational capacities was missing in most of these cases. Developing such indicators for intangible characteristics may be difficult but not impossible.

10.3 IMPLICATIONS FOR NORTHERN NGOs

Becoming seriously involved in strengthening local partner organisations can have considerable implications for Northern NGOs and their relations with their partners. Establishing effective capacity building programmes is a significant undertaking which requires not only that NGOs develop certain organisational capacities and facilitation skills, but may also lead Northern NGOs to rethink their long-term role in development.

Capacity building is empowerment by another name. It entails a redefinition of donor-recipient partnerships, and implies a more equitable balance of power between Northern and Southern NGOs. Sensitive power issues are involved and NGOs must be aware of some of the ethical dilemmas of intervening in an autonomous partner organisations. Some of these key issues will be briefly explored below.

Skills and Capacities

Designing and implementing effective capacity building programmes presupposes a thorough understanding of management and organisational issues. Most Northern NGOs at present lack in-house the skills to become proficient in building organisational capacity. As Northern NGOs become more involved in supportive and advisory roles, their skills and staff profiles must adapt to suit these changing functions.

NGOs will require staff with facilitation skills and management experience. Some changes in NGO staff composition are already occurring, as NGOs increasingly hire staff with previous commercial experience and MBAs, rather than the traditional pattern of agronomists or development studies graduates.

The changes occurring in the NGO sector are as yet an instinctive response to changing circumstances rather than a conscious decision to reformulate functions and acquire new capacities. In the coming years, Northern NGOs will need to be aware of these trends and consider if their current capacities will be suitable and sufficient in the medium to long term.

Partnership

NGOs have wholeheartedly adopted the rhetoric of partnership and of the devolution of power to the South. Translating this rhetoric into reality, as ever, is far more difficult. The concept of 'partnership' is both overused and poorly defined, and tends to obscure an important reality – conditions and priorities are set by donors and Northern NGOs who control financial resources. While many agencies use the term partnership, this in fact cloaks the unequal nature inherent in the relationship between donor and recipient.

Performance-related capacity building is only the first step in a genuine partnership. Subsequent stages of the relationship involve working toward the growing autonomy of the partner NGO, and expanding its capacity to act without external support. If capacity building is in fact empowerment, then it must be accompanied by a process which allows Southern NGOs greater responsibility for setting the development agenda, defining priorities and negotiating funding terms and conditions. Southern NGOs must be assisted to become strong and autonomous, by engaging in productive relations with other organisations, developing a degree of financial self-sufficiency and increasing their negotiating ability with governments.

Capacity building and empowerment require a shift in Northern NGOs' attitude towards partners from a directive to a facilitative approach. Northern NGOs' must evolve from being supervisors and auditors, which characterises their current funding roles, to facilitators and advisors. In the long term, partnerships should evolve from this teacher/tutor relationship to a mutually beneficial and supportive alliance of equals.

Some Northern NGOs are seeking to put the concepts of partnership and empowerment into practice. One way partnership is being advanced is through reformulating the funding practices which impose Northern conditions on Southern partners. Earlier chapters discussed a variety of ways in which this can be achieved, including flexible funding, negotiating funding conditions, ensuring partner input on key issues facing Northern NGOs, and moving beyond strictly project-tied funding.

Ethical Dilemmas of Intervening in Partner NGOs

This study has thus far strongly advocated the need for Northern NGOs to engage in capacity building for their Southern partners. As argued above, capacity building can be a useful tool for deepening and enriching partnerships between Northern and Southern NGOs. Yet, there are ethical and power issues involved which must be recognised. The unequal power basis of the two partners is in fact reflected in the phrase 'capacity building', which implies the subordinate role of the Southern NGO whose capacity is to be built – presumably by a Northern agency with capacity.

Capacity building and organisational development interventions can impinge on the sovereignty of Southern NGOs. There is a fine line between helping a partner to develop new management systems and policies as it sees fit, and imposing changes that may not be fully accepted or desired. This pressure may be unintentional. What may be a mere suggestion by a donor NGO to undergo a capacity building process may be perceived by the recipient NGO as an implicit threat to withhold funding if changes are not made. Northern NGOs must be aware that Southern NGOs may feel unable to say no to their funding partner.

Engaging in capacity building encourages NGOs to become openly critical about the capacities of their partners. If offered constructively within the framework of an open and honest relationship, this can be a catalyst for positive changes and improvement. It could be suggested, however, that there are sensitive, internal aspects of organisational culture which should remain private and not subject to outside interference. It is a useful exercise for Northern NGOs to consider how they would react if official donors attempted to gain influence over their internal functions.

Related questions exist regarding the appropriateness and capacity of Northern NGOs to intervene directly in their partner organisations. Generalist staff of Northern NGOs are being asked to design capacity building programmes, even though they may lack an understanding of the complexities of organisations and may not have a firm grasp of management issues. Most

Northern NGOs have not acquired the knowledge and understanding of management issues that is a necessary prerequisite for effective capacity building.

Capacity building and organisational development need to be engaged in with caution as inappropriate intervention can be both disruptive and damaging. For these reasons, Northern NGOs must be aware of the potential dangers and ensure that the leading force in setting priorities and identifying problems is the recipient NGO.

Institutionalising Support Structures for NGOs

If capacity building services are better left to specialist organisations, then what roles should Northern NGOs play in strengthening local NGO sectors? This study has argued that in addition to offering support to Southern partners, Northern NGOs should contribute to the institutional development of the NGO sector as a whole. Southern NGOs will be strengthened if they have systems and structures which ensure ongoing access to information, training and other support services.

Northern NGOs and donors concerned with the African NGO sector in the long term must ensure the adequate provision of capacity building services. The shortage of locally available specialist support for NGOs, both in management and technical issues, limits the opportunities for effective capacity building programmes. Rather than attempting to develop these skills in house, Northern NGOs and official donors should seek to strengthen the capacity of local service providers, such as NGO support organisations and local consultants.

10.4 CONCLUSION: CHANGING NGO ROLES IN DEVELOPMENT

Patterns in international aid flows are changing dramatically as Southern NGOs begin to attract a growing proportion of aid resources. Do these trends foreshadow a sharper division of labour, with Southern NGOs largely assuming the operational roles in development? As the number of strong and effective Southern NGOs continues to grow, there will be less justification for Northern NGOs to undertake operational roles in projects, apart from relief and emergency work. Prioritising capacity building serves to reinforce this division of labour. As Northern NGOs play supportive roles and engage earnestly in empowering their partners, they tacitly acknowledge that the active, direct roles in grassroots development should in future be performed by local actors and organisations, rather than through foreign intervention.

A new division of labour does not imply the demise of the Northern NGO, but may in fact prompt the development of a more mature and far-sighted NGO sector in the North. As they move away from direct operational roles, to 'third generation' process strategies, Northern NGOs are attempting to address the macro-level structural factors which perpetuate poverty. They must consider the national institutional framework of developing countries, and also take seriously educational and lobbying roles in their own countries. Educating their constituents and governments, leading to a more conducive international policy environment may be one role through which Northern NGOs can make a significant impact. These niches have yet to be fully explored and exploited.

Becoming proficient in capacity building may also be essential for their survival. The current trend of official donors funding Southern NGOs directly has led many to question the long-term relevance of Northern NGOs. Are they *en route* to becoming merely costly intermediaries in the aid system? As donors consider the direct funding of Southern agencies, Northern NGOs must demonstrate a 'value added' component to their work. They must prove that they are a channel of information and skills in addition to being a conduit for financial resources. In this new development agenda, their management and capacity building skills may become as important as their technical skills have been in the past. If 'partnership' is to be more than a funding relationship and contribute to the development of local capacity, then donors will recognise the comparative advantage of using Northern NGOs as intermediaries. If not, Northern NGOs may receive an ever-diminishing proportion of aid resources.

Bibliography

Albrecht, Karl. 1983. *Organization Development: a Total System Approach to Positive Change in any Business Organization.* Prentice Hall, Englewood Cliffs, New Jersey.

Amenuvor, Besa. 1993. *Improving the Internal Functioning of Micro and Small Enterprise Associations.* Paper prepared for, National Workshop UNECA Project on the Promotion of the Informal Sector for Development in Africa, Accra, Ghana, November 16-17.

APT Design and Development 1990. *Proposal to the Commissioners of the European Communities: Assistance to Small Scale and Cottage Industries in Uganda.* APT Design and Development. (unpublished report).

Berry, Sara. S. 1986. 'Economic Change in Contemporary Africa' in Martin and O'Meara (eds.) 1986.

Brews, Alan, 1994. *The Capacity Building Debate.* Olive Information Service, Durban, (unpublished report).

Butler, Richard J. and David C. Wilson. 1990. *Managing Voluntary and Non-Profit Organizations: Strategy and Structure.* Routledge, London.

Campbell, Piers. 1986. *Organizational Problems of NGOs.* ICVA, Management Training Modules

– 1989. *Institutional Development: Basic Principles and Strategies.* ICVA, Geneva. (unpublished report).

Carroll, Thomas. 1992. *Intermediary NGOs: The Supporting Link in Grassroots Development.* Kumarian Press, West Hartford Conn.

Clayton, Andrew (ed). 1994. *Governance, Democracy and Conditionality: What Role for NGOs?* INTRAC, Oxford.

Devereux, Stephen, Henry Pares and John Best. 1987. *Credit and Savings for Development.* Oxfam, Oxford.

Drucker, Peter. 1990. *Managing the NonProfit Organization: Principles and Practices.* HarperCollins, New York.

Eade, Deborah and Suzanne Williams. 1995. *The Oxfam Handbook of Development and Relief.* Oxfam, Oxford.

Edgcomb, Elaine and James Cawley, eds. 1993. *An Institutional Guide for Enterprise Development Organizations.* PACT Publications, New York.

Esman, Milton J. and Norman T. Uphoff. 1984. *Local Organizations: Intermediaries in Rural Development*. Cornell University Press, Ithaca and London.

Fowler, Alan, Piers Campbell, and Brian Pratt. 1992. *Institutional Development and NGOs in Africa: Policy Perspectives for European Development Agencies*. INTRAC, Oxford.

Fowler, Alan. 1990. What is Different About Managing Non-Government Organisations (NGOs) Involved in Third World Development? *NGO Management. No. 12,* ICVA, Geneva. January-March.

– 1992. Prioritizing Institutional Development: A New Role for NGO Centres for Study and Development. International Institute for Environment and Development, *Gatekeeper Series No. 35.* London.

Gibson, Alan and Mark Havers. 1994. *The Role of Small Business Membership Organisations (SBMOS) in Small Enterprise Development*. Overseas Development Group, Durham University Business School, (unpublished report).

Handy, Charles. 1990. *Understanding Voluntary Organizations*. Penguin Books, London.

Helmsing, A.H.J. and Th. Kolstee. 1993. *Small Enterprises and Changing Policies: Structural Adjustment, Financial Policy and Assistance Programmes in Africa*. Intermediate Technology Publications, London.

Harper, Malcolm. 1984. *Small Businesses in the Third World: Guidelines for Practical Assistance*. Intermediate Technology Publications, London.

Hurley, Donnacadh. 1990. *Income Generation Schemes for the Urban Poor.* Oxfam, Oxford.

INTRAC. 1993. *INTRAC Organisational Assessment Främework*. Intrac, Oxford, (unpublished report).

– 1994. *INTRAC Training Course Materials*. INTRAC, Oxford (unpublished report).

James, Rick. 1994a. Strengthening the Capacity of Southern NGO Partners: A Survey of Current Northern NGO Approaches'. *INTRAC Occasional Papers Series*. Vol.1, no.5.

– 1994b. *Capacity Building of Small Enterprise Development Agencies in Kenya: A Proposal to the British Council*. INTRAC, Oxford, (unpublished report).

Kiggundu, Moses N. 1989. *Managing Organizations in Developing Countries: An Operational and Strategic Approach*. Kumarian Press, West Hartford Conn.

Korten, David C. 1987. 'Third Generation NGO Strategies: A Key to People-Centred Development'. *World Development*. Vol. 15, supplement.

Levitsky, Jacob (ed.). 1989. *Microenterprises in Developing Countries*. Intermediate Technology Publications, London.

– 1993. Credit Guarantee Funds and Mutual Guarantee Systems. *Small Enterprise Development Journal*. Vol. 4, no. 2. (June).

– 1993b. Private Sector Organizations and Support for Small and Microenterprises. See Helmsing and Kolstee 1993.

Mann, Charles K., Merilee S. Grindle and Parker Shipton. 1989. *Seeking Solutions: Framework and Cases for Small Enterprise Development Programs*. Kumarian Press. West Hartford, Conn.

Marsden, David, Peter Oakley and Brian Pratt. 1994. *Measuring the Process: Guidelines for Evaluating Social Development*. INTRAC, Oxford.

Martin, Phyllis M. and Patrick O'Meara (eds.) 1986. *Africa*. Indiana University Press, Bloomington.

Moore, Mick, Sheelagh Stewart and Ann Hudock. 1994. *Institution Building as a Development Assistance Method; A Review of Literature and Ideas*. Report to the Swedish International Development Authority. Institute of Development Studies, Brighton, (unpublished report).

Novib. 1990. *Strengthening Organisations for Self-Supporting Development*. Novib, The Hague.

Nowak, Maria. 1989. 'The Role of Microenterprises in Rural Industrialization in Africa.' see Levitsky (ed.). 1989.

Olson, Mancur. 1965. *The Logic of Collective Action*. Harvard University Press, Cambridge, Mass.

Otero, Maria and Elisabeth Rhyne (eds.). *The New World of Microenterprise Finance: Building Healthy Financial Institutions for the Poor*. Kumarian Press. West Hartford, Conn.

Piza Lopez, Eugenia and Candida March. 1991. Gender Considerations in Economic Enterprises: Report of a Workshop held in the Philippines, November 1990. *Oxfam Discussion Paper #2*.

Sahley, Caroline. 1991. *Prospects and Options for Income Generation Programmes in Low Income Areas of Lima Peru*. INCA, London. (mimeo).

– 1995. 'NGO Support for Small Business Associations: A Participatory Approach to Small Enterprise Development'. *Community Development Journal*. January.

Saith, Ashwani. 1992. *The Rural Non-Farm Economy: Process and Policies.* International Labour Office, Geneva.

Siddle, David and Ken Swindell. 1990. *Rural Change in Tropical Africa: From Colonies to Nation-States.* Basil Blackwell, Oxford.

Tengey, Wilbert. 1993. *Objectives, Approach and Implementation of the Informal Sector Project (The Ghana Experience).* Report presented to the National Workshop on the Promotion of the Informal Sector, Accra, Ghana. 16–17 November 1993.

UN-ECA. 1993a. *Promotion of the Informal Sector for Development in Africa. Phase 1 – Pilot Assistance to Ghana and Cote D'Ivoire.* Address of the UNECA Representative at the Opening Ceremony of the National Workshop on the Promotion of the Informal Sector. Accra, Ghana. 16 November 1993.

– 1993b. *Draft Constitution: Association of Small Scale Industries.* Document prepared by National Steering Committee for the National Workshop on the Promotion of the Informal Sector. Accra, Ghana. 16 November 1993.

Uphoff, Norman. 1986. *Local Institutional Development: An Analytical Sourcebook with Cases.* Kumarian Press, West Hartford.

– 1992. Local Institutions and Participation for Sustainable Development. International Institute for Environment and Development, *Gatekeeper Series* No. 31. London.

WUS. 1994. *WUS Directory of Training.* World University Service, London.

The INTRAC Management and Policy Series

Institutional Development and NGOs in Africa: Policy Perspectives for European Development Agencies
Alan Fowler, with Piers Campbell and Brian Pratt, 1993
ISBN 1–897748–00–0, pp52
£7.95 +p+p

Institutional Development (ID) is recognised as an important element in projects and programmes dedicated to the sustainable alleviation of poverty, the promotion of gender equity, and the achievment of social justice for marginalised populations. This publication provides an overview of NGO ID in the context of sub-Saharan Africa.

* * * * *

Governance, Democracy and Conditionality: What Role for NGOs?
Andrew Clayton (ed.), 1994
ISBN 1–897748–01–9, pp136
£9.95 +p+p

This publication addresses the issues of good governance and conditionality from the perspective of both Northern and Southern NGOs. Case studies are included that draw on the experiences of NGOs in Africa, Asia and Latin America, and cover a wide range of issues concerning the role of NGOs in civil society, advocacy, legal reform and democracy movements.

* * * * *

Measuring the Process: Guidelines for Evaluating Social Development
David Marsden, Peter Oakley and Brian Pratt, 1994
ISBN 1–897748–06–X, pp178
£12.95 +p+p

Based on an international workshop which brought together both practitioners and academics, this book is intended primarily as a practical guide for undertaking the evaluation of social development projects. It combines a theoretical overview of the concepts involved with insights into planning and implementation of evaluation. Three substantial case studies of evaluation are provided from Colombia, India and Zimbabwe, as well as an extensive literature review.